Corporate Reputation

Corporate Reputation

Managing
the
New Strategic Asset

John Smythe,
Colette Dorward
Jerome Reback

CENTURY
BUSINESS

First published in Great Britain in 1992 by
Century Business
An imprint of Random House UK Limited
20 Vauxhall Bridge Road, London SW1V 2SA

Random House Australia (Pty) Limited
20 Alfred Street, Milsons Point, Sydney
New South Wales 2061, Australia

Random House New Zealand Limited
18 Poland Road, Glenfield
Auckland 10, New Zealand

Random House South Africa (Pty) Limited
PO Box 337, Bergvlei, South Africa

Set in Bembo by Edna A. Moore 𝙁 Tek-Art, Croydon, Surrey
Printed and bound in Great Britain by
Mackays of Chatham PLC, Chatham, Kent

British Library Cataloguing in Publication Data
A catalogue record for this book is available from the British Library

ISBN 0-7126-5059-8

Companies, institutions and other organizations wishing to make bulk
purchases of this title or any other Century Business publication should
contact:

Direct Sales Manager
Century Business
Random Century House
20 Vauxhall Bridge Road
London SW1V 2SA

Fax: 071-828 6681

Contents

Acknowledgements

The authors would like to thank all those who made publication of this book possible, particularly past and present employees of Smythe Dorward Lambert, our clients and others who have helped to make our business a success.

Particular thanks to Jane Wilby, John Harben, Amanda Rosenfeld, to all our families for putting up with it, and to Wally Olins and Armand Hammer who taught us that conviction is half the battle!

Foreword

Those of us who believe that competitive advantage, in the corporate world, is becoming less a question of what a firm *does* and more a question of what a firm *is*, have a problem.

We find it easy enough to stimulate a dinner party interest in the basic idea that companies have personalities and that these help determine how successful they are. But we find it hard to persuade managers and the City, that anything of practical use can come of it.

The general view seems to be that, although the idea of the living company, with appetites, instincts, prejudices and passions, is an engaging fancy with which to while away an idle moment or two, it should never be permitted to distract the attention of managers from the 'bottom line'.

The irony of this 'macho' appetite for hard figures, and the 'bottom line', is that modern financial statements – where the bottom line is supposed to live – are about as distant from reality as pre-Copernican cosmology. They are stuffed full of the artefacts of the accounting method, and are very unreliable guides for the husbandry of corporate assets.

One only has to remember the huge premiums over book value and market value paid for brand-rich companies in the 1980s to have profound reservations about the accuracy with which accountants and the market measure corporate worth.

That enlightened managers know that the new philosophers of 'soft' assets have a point, is evidenced by frequent remarks in annual statements to the effect, for example, that 'Our reputation is our greatest asset'. But all too often, such references are revealed as ritual declarations, constrained by the exigencies of the company's primary duty to increase earnings per share.

It is as if the 'soft' asset, though it is beginning to be taken seriously, has yet to be taken into account.

What's needed, and what this book helps to provide, is a way of reconciling the hard and the soft, so that the latter can take its rightful place on the agenda of a company's highest strategic councils. The soft and hard need a common language and a common methodology if the full potential of the latter to enrich the former is to be realized.

In the pages that follow, John Smythe, Colette Dorward and Jerome Reback describe a systematic approach to reputation management that goes a long way towards the creation of just such a common language and methodology. They have provided a way of thinking about reputation that is consistent with and, more important, can be readily accommodated by conventional strategic thinking.

They have built a bridge, in this book, between theory and practice, over which I expect much animated traffic to pass.

And because they are experienced, professional consultants, there is nothing academic or high-falutin' about the way they tackle these difficult and subtle issues. They have built their bridge out of familiar concepts and practical techniques and, in so doing, have taken some of the mystique out of the 'soft' debate.

It is often the fate of new ideas to be misunderstood, and to be dismissed as impractical. They cannot begin to exert real influence, and challenge the old orthodoxy, until their practical implications are described and explored. Smythe, Dorward and Reback will take those who read this book a long way towards a full understanding of how corporate reputation can be managed and nurtured, in a strategic way to deliver competitive advantage.

In an uncertain future, there is one thing I am sure of, and that is that companies who care about their reputations will do better than those who do not.

Tom Lloyd
Financial Journalist and Consultant

Introduction

The central idea of this book has been tested time and again by its authors. It has also been obscured by decades when businesses have been absorbed with advertising and public relations, as if they were some kind of 'technology' which communicates an image to the outside world.

The truth is that the reputation of an organization is much more powerful than its image, and is all about *internal* relationships inside the organization and among its employees.

We argue that a good reputation can and should become a new strategic asset.

We explain how successful organizations are learning to manage their reputation, and why all organizations – if they are to thrive – must learn to give the same attention to this as they do to finance, production and other core functions.

We explain why everybody in the organization is responsible for its reputation and how everyone can find a role sustaining it.

The book is divided into five parts. In Part One, *A new strategic asset*, we explore what reputation means. In Part Two, *Part of the management process*, we ask whether cultures can be changed and show how to go about changing them. Parts Three and Four look at *Managing internal and external communication* and Part Five looks at how to plan this new area of corporate communications.

We believe that a single strong theme sounds through the pages that follow. It is that everyone in an organization has a story to tell, and that good communication is about co-ordinating these stories into a coherent whole.

The effort is worth it, because corporate 'myth' – the idea of the organization – *can* be promoted and managed.

Part One

A
New
Strategic Asset

1
What is Reputation?

The importance of reputation, how it is different from the old-fashioned idea of 'image' – and how companies which nurture their reputation are the ones which will succeed in a changing consumer climate.

The age of the ethical consumer has arrived. Ethical consumers do not leave their consciences at the door of the store when looking for the best deal. They want to know who is behind the familiar name on the product. They want to know whether the parent organization is making unsavoury investments in another country. Or what political platforms it supports. Or what stances it takes on *their* issues.

Companies have been quick to recognize this new attitude, and many have notoriously tried to cash in on the consumer's awareness of environmental issues. But their early attempts to slap 'green' labels on products which were otherwise exactly the same as before have given way to a real determination to understand public opinion. At best that allows them to take advantage of changing attitudes: at the very least it helps them avoid the threat of a consumer boycott.

The British supermarket chain Tesco used to be famous for piling it high and selling it cheap. But in the 1980s, it built a new reputation on the basis of a new – and more profitable –

understanding of this new breed of ethical consumer.

Tesco achieved this by using market research which explored changes in lifestyle and social trends. It listened and learned and then took calculated risks. It supported the growers of organic food until the produce was able to command a premium on the shelves.

This was a brave pre-emption of public opinion and it is paying off for Tesco and its suppliers. But it is also changing the way people understand the company. They can see that the displays of organic produce reflect careful thinking beyond the charade of green labelling.

This kind of enlightened self-interest is not new. The corporations built by visionary industrialists like Lever and Cadbury, who created decent homes for their workforces at Port Sunlight and Bourneville, remain in existence. The Victorian profiteers whom Dickens wrote about in *Hard Times* have disappeared.

All successful organizations which span the generations share a clear sense of what makes them useful. They have strong values which shape the behaviour of their employees. The best of the founder's visions are retained, and everybody associated with the business understands them. There is a collective conscience.

It is sobering to remember just how fragile organizations are. A look back at *Fortune* magazine's roll-call of the top 500 American corporations shows that two thirds of the companies listed in the 1956 edition have disappeared. Only 29 of the 100 biggest US firms are still there, one working life later, and only 27 of the top 100 non-American firms. This is a cautionary reminder to refresh the **collective memory** of why employees are still collecting their pay cheques.

Employees and outsiders alike want to know that the corporation stands for certain ideas. These will include financial gain but will be much broader than the profit motive alone. People prefer to identify with this type of corporation rather than with those that make no effort to establish relationships with consumers, employees and communities.

For many corporations, this means learning new social skills. The basis of the good relationships they need to build is often nothing more fancy than good manners. Bad manners can cost a fortune, especially when – as in the USA – going to law is still often seen as the best way to negotiate between the interests of the corporation and its neighbours. When an organization introduces a contentious pay deal, or tries to build a new plant in somebody else's back yard, good manners are probably the best basis for managing relationships – and consequently for achieving goals.

The problem is that good manners do not come without pain. Many corporations have become too used to getting their own way and dictating terms, particularly to their employees. Not any more. Western organizations now need to learn corporate courtesy and communicate with the people on whom they depend. The organizations which cannot or will not build this kind of dialogue will fail.

What has been happening in the USA, where the social relevance of corporations has led to ever more stringent yardsticks of acceptability, makes this all the more urgent. The movement arose out of a much more pernicious Political Correctness – the so-called 'PC' – by which advocates try to ensure that their ideology becomes the accepted wisdom. American professors who espouse 'incorrect' dogmas are hounded and ostracized until they either defer, quit or are subject to a politically-inspired 'coup'.

The movement has expanded from campus into community, and is championing a social exorcism of 'Politically Incorrect' behaviour like drinking, smoking and holding the 'wrong' views. At one level this can be seen as people power harnessing a well-organized style of lobbying. But it can also be seen as the start of a process which allows one social group to dominate and even suppress another.

Whether PC is a fad or not, it has already taught more benign lobby groups to marshal their cases more effectively against organizations and the state.

The implications of this go very deep. Whether managers like it or not, managing the differences between the organization and its employees, customers, users and the community is set to become a very sophisticated business. Marketing an organization can no longer rely on creating a glossy image. Corporations need to learn about what drives the decisions of their customers. They have to take into account what these groups expect of them, and decide whether their own behaviour is good enough to guarantee their future.

It also means:

- The traditional public relations role must be buried for ever, and

- The promise offered by the organization to the outside world must match reality.

Because of this, responsibility for communication can no longer be relegated to the hapless spokesperson. The traditional outward-looking role of public relations must be transformed so that it becomes central to the management of business. This means developing a new set of skills which helps the organization to understand all the groups with which it deals. It also means building up two-way communication with these groups, rather than just delivering the organization's message to them.

The term 'public relations' has become associated with the unthinking passing on of corporate propaganda, and it is now fashionable to characterize spokespeople as supine morons with no opinions of their own. The correct targets are the faceless leaders who hide behind their useless press releases – leaders who are simply not able to handle the organizations' relationships with the media, employees or others, and who always seem to have a good reason for making 'no comment'.

In some corporations the cover-up has become so ingrained that they are rationalizing activities which have long been regarded as unacceptable. The trouble with cover-ups is that they must go on and on: once started they become the guiding principle which undermines the entire management process. The way the late Robert Maxwell controlled the 'truth' in his companies led, ultimately, to disastrous results.

Corporations can be judged by the style of their communications. Where they are defensive, weak or deliberately misleading, it is almost always a sign of a defensive or introspective management team. It may also indicate that the organization has something to hide – or worse, nothing to say.

Often it takes a public crisis to expose the real values of a corporation. At that moment, all the beautifully crafted mission statements and the carefully prepared contingency plans will confirm that the organization's values are really as they are advertised – or not, as the case may be. In the heat of a crisis, people don't reach for the newly written mission or value statement: they are guided by ingrained values which have been at work down the years.

When the oil platform Piper Alpha exploded in the North Sea in July 1989, Occidental's 89-year-old chairman Dr Armand Hammer flew overnight from Los Angeles, fronted a score of media interviews and *accepted responsibility*.

When a British Midland Boeing 737 crashed on an English motorway yards from the runway at East Midlands Airport in 1989, BM chief executive Michael Bishop was there within hours to take the rap in the searching lights of worldwide television crews.

The management of the *Exxon Valdez* ecological disaster in Alaska's Prince William Sound was less successful.

Every organization must treat its reputation as an asset which requires constant development and careful handing down from generation to generation. That reputation is the sum of the corporation's daily actions, and it will determine whether recruits will join, consumers will buy, and journalists and legislators give it the benefit of the doubt.

So the development of the corporation's **collective conscience and memory** must become the responsibility of every manager. There need to be training and development programmes which support them in this role.

But the management of reputation also needs a new discipline with a new, meaningful name to distinguish it from the old-style propaganda of externally-orientated public relations officers.

The new function has a holistic role. Its prime aim is to open a dialogue with everyone the organization deals with, not least employees, to negotiate goals which are satisfactory to everyone.

Marketing, human resources and corporate communication departments must accept that they are all part of *one* process – communicating the organization's reputation. They have no other function except to make the organization acceptable and useful to employees, customers and society at large.

A vast proportion of communication budgets still goes towards promotion to the world outside, often via advertising, and as a result marketing chiefs are often more powerful than their counterparts in corporate communications and human resources. More often than not, image leads reality by the nose.

The corporate image is invariably invented by outsiders whose thinking is usually concerned with the fantasy world of aspirational advertising for perfume or condoms. Image, like perfumes and sex, often disappoints.

The new approach, on the other hand, has to take account of the internal world. To use a religious term, it aims to create a 'covenant' with employees, customers and the community. This is more valuable, but more difficult, than managing image by itself.

The following pages are a guide to building this new covenant.

SUMMARY – WHAT IS REPUTATION?

- A corporation's values are kept alive in a collective memory of its behaviour, with its leaders responsible for keeping the vision of its founders fresh.

- Good manners are the basis of good communication.

- The traditionally defensive role of public relations no longer serves a useful role.

- There is a need for a new area of management which can open dialogue with employees, communities and other groups.

- Image must not be allowed to lead reality by the nose.

- Reputation is a core management activity.

2
Managing the Asset

How to recognize the pitfalls of managing a reputation, when the stories people tell about you are much more powerful than the old-fashioned tools of management by memo and a PR-led external profile.

Strong cultures, like those of Delta Airlines, Marks & Spencer, IBM or British Rail, all provide people with similar experiences of working for them or dealing with them.

All have reputations which are widely perceived and commonly experienced. This is because they have a large number of customers, and most of us know somebody who has dealt with them or read about them in the press and absorbed their own propaganda. Nor do they have to be big companies to have a reputation which is widely perceived: small organizations have equally potent reputations in their own worlds. English country pubs, small town American diners, French village cafés make their own big noises locally.

HOW REPUTATION IS SPREAD TO EMPLOYEES

The main experiences which have a powerful impact on staff include the following:

- The experience of joining the company and induction.

- The impact of training.

- The influence and example of other staff and supervisors.

- The setting of personal objectives and the company's appraisal process.

This list is not exhaustive. The diagram illustrates the range of different influences which come to bear on a recruit during his or her career with the organization.

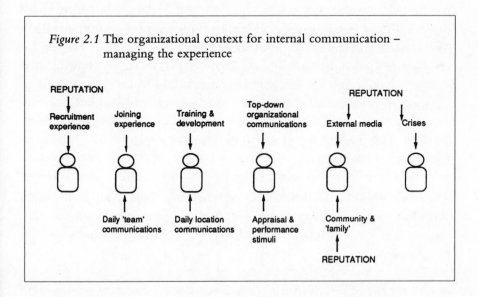

Figure 2.1 The organizational context for internal communication – managing the experience

Before applying for the job, this new employee might have been attracted by the organization's reputation. Having joined the company, our recruit will rapidly be exposed to its procedures and values. Some organizations take this to extremes. Lex Services, a UK-based mini conglomerate, used to make a formal point of asking if potential recruits could 'live up to' the corporate mission statement before their application would be considered seriously.

But the most powerful induction experience waits for the recruit to arrive on the shop floor or place of work. Then the team they will be working with will quickly set the tone and put our recruit 'right'. The organization can redress the balance by pulling employees out of the workplace and sending them on training courses, or by the annual appraisal, special programmes like quality improvement or messages of exhortation by the company chairman. Yet all the time, the organization is having to compete for the employee's attention with newspaper stories about the company, the views of family or friends, or statements made by politicians or trade unionists.

To make things even more difficult for themselves, most corporate leaders fail to co-ordinate the programmes which are at their disposal to influence employees. Specialist functions like marketing, human resources, quality and strategic planning, are often running programmes which are independent – even conflict-ing. It hardly needs saying that, often, these programmes, set up by unco-ordinated departments, are a confusing waste of resources. If it is to work well, internal communication has to be planned just as rigorously as companies plan their customer marketing.

HOW REPUTATION IS SPREAD TO OUTSIDERS

The same rigour also needs to be applied to managing relationships with key external groups, like customers, politicians and the media. Reputation is transmitted to them by experiences such as the following:

- The kind of relationships they have with the organization – and how consistent they are.

- Experience of specific transactions, e.g. buying a hamburger.

- Messages from the organization's brochures or, more interestingly, other literature, such as forms and standard letters – which are always a giveaway as to what the organization *really* thinks of its customers.

- Messages from advertising and promotional materials.

- Experience of entering the organization's offices or sales outlets.

Reputation is passed on by nearly everybody. Even people who have no direct relationship with the organization sometimes influence those who do. So it is absurd to separate the internal communication from the external: another reason for making sure communications are planned and co-ordinated as a core managerial discipline.

Communication is a primary process: we live *in* communication, rather than standing *outside* it. When beliefs are challenged, it is those stories with mythic power that sustain beliefs. The reason why so few managements co-ordinate their top down messages is that they see 'communications' as a toolbox, or some kind of odourless fluid that can simply be channelled with a corporate video or a new staff publication. Yet the power of the stories which circulate outside their immediate control – stories with mythic power – are almost infinitely greater than these.

FOUR TYPES OF COMPANY

Smythe Dorward Lambert's 1989 study *Your Employees, Your Edge in the 1990s* investigated 54 European corporations and identified four broad categories of company culture.

These are:

- Entrepreneurial organizations.

- Stable, institutionalized organizations.

- Contrived cultures.

- Rapidly-changing organizations.

This is not a definitive list of organizational types, but it may be useful to help you think about what kind of communications prevail in your own organization.

Entrepreneurial organizations
Here lines of communication tend to be so short and the vision so clear that internal communication is almost a 'natural' activity. People tend to know where they fit and what is happening day by day. There is little hoarding of information.

But when an entrepreneurial company becomes larger and more complex, it can be difficult to keep this communication so open and fluid. Often a human resource or corporate communications function will begin to develop, which is expected to capture and spread the essence of this culture. But however carefully they are designed, these new management systems and techniques tend to be undermined by an innate distrust of bureaucracy and overheads.

Stable or institutionalized organizations
Typically these are companies which have enjoyed relatively stable periods, free of upheaval from regulations or new market pressures. Many have become bureaucratic, highly complex, multi-product companies which are widely spread geographically and culturally diverse. Life in these organizations tends to be structured and people are very conscious of status. Meetings are formal and information, where it is shared at all, is heavily sanitized.

Contrived Cultures
Marks & Spencer, McDonalds and Mars are typical examples of these. They have a powerful set of expectations about behaviour which are shared internally, and often known about outside through the power of corporate myth.

Many of these organizations were founded by someone with firm views about ethics or behaviour which have been passed on in this strong culture – and sustained by employee training and a clear corporate identity. In the best of them, empire-building and information hoarding is usually restricted by a culture which is deliberately made to be as open as possible. Despite their often large size, some of the positive aspects of communication in entrepreneurial organizations also apply to them.

The Rapidly Changing Organization

The fourth type of organization may once have been stable, but is suddenly having to make major strategic or cultural changes for economic, social or political reasons.

Determined managements will probably have realized that they must carry employees along with them and will have tried to communicate the new strategy. Employees may find themselves subjected to a variety of techniques, including cascade briefings, imaginative printed information, videos and roadshows. We explore these ideas further in Part Three.

WHEN CHANGE GOES WRONG

Organizations which survive their creators successfully tend to have a clear shared sense of purpose, underpinned by a set of values which are inculcated into staff until the day they retire. The process is controlled by management and not by the subversive counter-culture of the canteen. The culture of organizations such as IBM and Federal Express have visibly survived the passing on of the management baton, as have equally strong non-corporate cultures such as the French Foreign Legion.

In other organizations, the prevailing culture may not always serve the customer best. In London's Metropolitan Police, the culture still rewards arrests rather than preventing crime. The Plus Programme being implemented by senior officers was set up after a cultural review by external consultants, and aims to redefine the relationship between London's police and the public. But the strength of the old role, essentially to gain personal status by 'nicking' as many villains as possible, means that the police are accepting the programme only very slowly.

Similar displays of strength of purpose can be found in all fields of human endeavour. While the board decides that the rules have changed, it can take years for the workforce to relinquish their old beliefs. Yet new objectives may be essential if – as in the case of the old state-owned steel businesses – they are to survive at all.

The new owners of British Steel, or any other concern whose role is being radically changed, cannot assume that this is just a matter of running a profitable company. More than most, these enterprises will need to remake the contract with their staff and the communities from which they have profited in the past.

The most common complaint of managers – whatever the reason for the change – is that they have too little time to bring everybody along with their plans. Yet they often behave as if their staff have telepathic powers, and are able to react immediately to the one page memo from senior management which sets out the new order.

The result is organizational trauma. The chief executive has a new set of financial imperatives and the rest of the organization is expected to drop ways of doing things which may have been valued by customers and communities, and to pick up new rules and practices with neither explanation nor context – and seldom any valid process of measurement which will tell them when they have got there.

THE EXAMPLE OF CEPSA

Managements and boards quickly forget how much effort went into making their existing reputation valuable. Big, sustainable and successful ideas take time to nurture. As the managing director of Spanish petrochemical giant Compania Española de Petroleos SA (CEPSA) put it: 'We expected our 6,000 staff to drop 60 years of ingrained practices with the issue of a memorandum which eloquently explained our first radical reorganization in all that time.'

A year later the board was asking itself why nothing had changed. We had conducted a series of discussions with the staff of CEPSA all over Spain as part of what was – in 1989 – the first programme of its kind in a Spanish company in the run up to that country's admission into the European Community.

CEPSA staff had been used to lifelong employment and gradual elevation up the corporate ladder in recognition of length of service. But the company's prospects in the EC included vigorous competition from foreign oil companies, which had been prevented from entering Spain's monopolized state oil sector.

To deal with the threat, consultants had advised the management team to make a series of organizational changes. An oil refinery in Tenerife, for example, would have to become much more involved with other sites around the country. The proposed integration of cherished 'baronies' like the Tenerife operation brought added tensions because of Spain's provincial rivalries, which reflect centuries of enmity. But there was no precedent to follow, which was why nothing changed.

We persuaded the company's management to conduct a staff survey and to use it to plan a nationwide debate about the changes. CEPSA's president Eugenio Marin Garcia-Mansilla conducted these debates himself, and soon a controversy had been ignited across the organization. 'As soon as I began to get resistance I knew that the message had begun to get through,' said Marin.

Too often leaders try to delegate the communication and implementation of change to frustrated specialists who know that they cannot win by glossy print alone. In an ingrained culture, a strong dose of constructive controversy has to be introduced before everyone starts to think through the consequences for their own jobs and their future careers.

CAN REPUTATION BE MANAGED?

The answer is yes. Reputation is managed intuitively by small organizations every day, because their proprietors instinctively know how to handle their customers.

Larger corporations attempt to manage their reputations by establishing commonly accepted ways of doing things. McDonalds, for example, tries to offer customers the same standard of service anywhere in the world. They lay down the 'right' way of doing things by processing their managers through the McDonalds University and by promoting a common marketing message. It is no accident that the McDonalds experience is as good in Moscow as it is in Kansas City or the Champs Elysées. The stories and experiences that create a reputation, when they are repeated time after time, *can* be managed.

But as we discussed earlier, there are many different ways of experiencing an organization. And changing or strengthening the reputation of an organization must inevitably embrace all these different aspects. It is not enough to fiddle with the projected image. It requires a process similar to the idea of Total Quality Management (TQM), because the responsibility belongs to everyone.

It also means that a senior manager needs to act as a high level 'sponsor' to keep the momentum going after the novelty has worn off.

But the management of reputation is subtly different to that of TQM. Failing to focus on quality may seriously affect the organization's ability to thrive, but it will probably be just one of a number of factors which influences its fate. With reputation, key decisions are being made about the organization – by customers or potential recruits – even before they come into direct contact with it. They hear the stories about other people's experiences.

Organizations are not able to do away with their reputations, however secretive they are. In fact the more secretive they become, the greater the number of stories or myths that get built up around them and the more likely that rivals, commentators and others will distort the 'reality'.

Nor is it any answer to substitute the word 'private' for 'secretive', as the family owners of Europe's C&A clothing chain store have always done. The Brenninkmeyers may enjoy the luxury of privacy and their employees may not care too much when trading is good, but what is the value of a 'secretive' reputation when times are bad or outside pressure groups threaten?

The sheer potential of managing this reputation is massively misunderstood. Corporations which have invested time and resources in active management have benefited from customer and employee loyalty. They have been accepted by vital outside groups – not the least of which are the shareholders – and have been supported by local communities and business regulators. But there are not many organizations which have done so.

SUMMARY – MANAGING THE ASSET

- Big and small organizations have equally potent reputations in their own worlds.

- Reputation is the sum of stories told about an organization.

- Employees are most powerfully influenced by:
  – Joining and induction experiences.
  – Training and development.
  – Example of peers and supervisors.
  – Appraisal processes.

- Communication is a primary process: we live *in* communication, rather than standing *outside* it.

- No organization can choose to do away with its reputation.

3
A Journey Inside
Two Organizations

How to tell an organization with a good reputation from the rest. We take a visitor's journey through two very different corporations.

This is the Reputation Diagram:

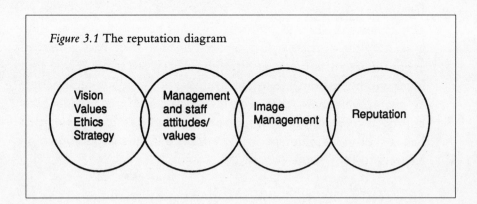

Figure 3.1 The reputation diagram

Vision
Values
Ethics
Strategy

Management
and staff
attitudes/
values

Image
Management

Reputation

Visiting the Good Company

Let us follow in the footsteps of a visitor setting foot inside a good company, and walk through the various aspects of corporate life which make up its reputation.

- **Vision, values, ethics and strategy**
  Visitors are able to glean a reasonably comprehensive – and in this case, consistent view about the organization from everyone they meet, by looking at what they do, how they are treated and how they carry out their business. A healthy and open debate seems to be constantly questioning the status quo. Similarly, if the visitor is able to interview a panel of outsiders who depend on the organization in some way, there is a remarkable degree of consistency.

- **Management and staff attitudes and values**
  Managers assure the visitor that employees are key assets. Time has clearly been spent working out how to involve people – for their own satisfaction as well as for the greater good of the organization. The staff think so too and their views are not only canvassed on a formal basis regularly but are listened to and acted upon.

- **Image management**
  Both management and staff are proud of how their organization is seen by the outside world, and are keen to keep that good will even if there are sometimes differences between them. The senior level will be responsible for communications, and several people at that level share this responsibility. There is a collegiate approach to planning programmes. Everybody in management has an obvious interest in the organization's reputation and expects to play some part in developing it.

  However small it is, the organization has a recognizable voice on the issues facing its own industry and may also be a visible player in the communities where it operates – though it is unlikely to give unthinkingly or condescendingly.

- **Reputation**
  The visitor is struck by a definite sense of purpose which seems to be common to everybody. The organization may not be universally liked – in fact passions may run high about some aspects of it. But on the whole it is respected and seems to tell the truth. The visitor has enjoyed the encounter and will remember the experience positively.

VISITING DISMAL PLC

Now let's follow the visitor to another organization – we'll call it Dismal PLC – which takes little interest in its reputation.

- **Vision, values and strategy**
  Our visitor can find much less common ground between managers, and people seem rather nervous about saying what they think. They seem to have had little involvement in questioning or developing the organization. The rules are said to be strict and seem to change a lot. Everybody laughs when the word 'values' is mentioned.

- **Management, staff attitudes and values**
  The personnel department is universally distrusted and a discussion with its head, if there is one, reveals a chiselling or even vengeful attitude.
  Management seem to meet as rarely as possible, apparently to save money. But staff regale the visitor with stories about how different managers hate each other and would rather 'screw up' than robustly negotiate their differences to produce a better product.

- **Image management**
  The ex-journalist running the despised PR department is expected to improve the image by issuing the occasional press release containing good news. But he can rarely persuade the chief executive to go 'on the record' with a journalist without a

promise that he can review the story before it appears. The organization is poorly regarded by most journalists.

The marketing director thinks that the abilities of her PR colleague are barely satisfactory. Neither are members of the ruling coalition. Together with the personnel manager, they are thought of as necessary functionaries.

- **Reputation**
  Our visitor finds that views of the organization are as varied as the number of people interviewed. Nobody seems particularly fond of it and two months later, the visitor can remember very little except a lingering sense of mediocrity.

The message of the Reputation Diagram is that managing reputation has to begin by setting out the organization's vision clearly. This might mean describing its niche in a market, or in the case of a non-commercial body, its useful role in society.

Its values need to be equally clear: those beliefs which teach people how to respond to different situations.

Finally there is the strategy: the practical plans which turn vision into achievement.

Only when all these have been defined can all employees know what is personally expected of them and the acceptable ways of doing their jobs. Once the vision, values and strategy are clearly set out in recruitment criteria, induction programmes and staff development – and are reinforced in the appraisal process – it then makes sense to tackle the formal image management process. The best organizations make sure they are delivering the same messages outside the organization via marketing and PR as they transmit internally.

For that reason, the people responsible for shaping the work environment and for communicating with the outside world have to work closely together and be integral members of the senior management team.

SUMMARY – A JOURNEY INSIDE TWO ORGANIZATIONS

Managing image must:

- Be tackled only after you have clearly articulated your vision, values and strategy.

- Take into account the values and attitudes of staff and management, otherwise no strategy can be sustained.

- Make sure that external promise matches inner reality.

- Involve all managers as part of the communication team.

Part Two

Part of the Management Process

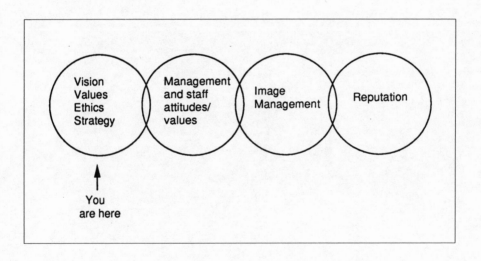

Vision Values Ethics Strategy — Management and staff attitudes/values — Image Management — Reputation

You are here

4
Managing Culture

**How can the 'culture' of an organization be managed as a
resource like any other business asset? Are corporate efforts to
clone the behaviour of employees beneficial in the long term?**

**A practical step-by-step guide to understanding the prevailing
ethos in your own organization, and how to manage change to
achieve company objectives.**

Changes are being forced on organizations which lead them, because
of changes in the world outside, to take a different approach to
managing their employees' attitudes to work. These changes reflect
shifts in both the changing market and the technology available to
the company but are also bound up with social and political changes
– as well as initiatives which come from inside.

Market Change
Now that people are increasingly interested in what an organization
stands for, major companies like the oil giant BP have to find ways
of responding.

BP is putting itself through a major change programme called
Project 2000, aimed at making the company more nimble-footed.
As part of this it was decided to re-equip key senior managers with

personal computers. Instead of choosing a supplier with a similar cultural style – IBM for example – BP opted for Apple Computers. The management team wanted to signal change in everything it did, and no computer company could have been more different to the old-style BP than the entrepreneurial Apple.

If anything, BP has been too successful. It set out to unravel the status-ridden hierarchies of the 'old' organization by removing power from formal departments and giving it to ad hoc work groups, but then found that people wanted to be involved in even the most minor decisions. Participation may have gone too far. The programme is now trying to find a way of involving people without everybody feeling they must be consulted on everything.

People's attitudes to work can be changed, but without careful handling the balance can sometimes swing too far for comfort. To avoid these pitfalls, change needs to be constantly updated.

This is one reason why managing change has become a prime role for management. But individual management teams are also having to come to terms with massive social changes which are having an impact just as important as changes in technology and competition.

Social Change

In Britain these social changes are particularly pronounced and can be represented as follows:

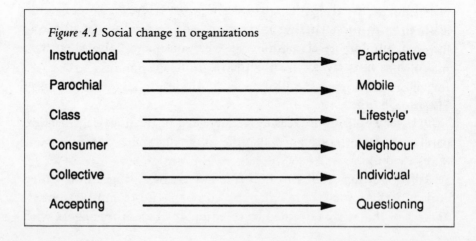

Figure 4.1 Social change in organizations

Instructional	Participative
Parochial	Mobile
Class	'Lifestyle'
Consumer	Neighbour
Collective	Individual
Accepting	Questioning

The British have become a more mobile people, and less inclined to hang on to class labels. They have used the revolution in corporate design to forge identities of their own, and are keen to question the policies and practices of organizations from which they are buying goods or services.

The changes to business life resulting from these social shifts have also been important. The British engineering group Dowty, which supplied most of the world's aircraft with their undercarriages, underwent a social remodelling under chief executive Tony Thatcher, whose reforms included sweeping away five layers of dining room on his arrival.

Nor was it very long ago since managers at the giant British insurance company Prudential would send memos to each other in Latin, and used impersonal phrases like 'it has been decided that' to spell out decisions. Until a recent campaign, use of the personal 'you' was avoided.

In the grain-growing county of Suffolk, beer brewers Greene King – one of Britain's most traditional family firms – still has a ruling which sees sandwiches served in the boardroom cut into triangles while the general canteen makes do with square cut. But even here, demands for more involvement from employees led to a radical programme which Tim Bridge, the current managing director, spearheaded himself.

A similar tendency – for employees to involve themselves – came to light during the recent battle for franchises in the British independent TV sector. London's Thames Television discovered an element of entrepreneurial flair in its midst as it prepared its bid. The librarian who archived the vast collection of filmed material had been making £200,000 or so for the company by responding to requests for short film clips and making a modest charge on his own initiative.

Thames realized that by enabling everybody to feel they had a part to play in making the company successful and relevant, it could make the station more profitable – and more satisfying to work for as well.

Political Change

The politically-inspired privatizations in British industry have resulted in a tendency on the part of newly privatized companies to reflect on their way of doing things. They have found themselves with new roles thrust on them, suddenly expected to behave as if they were operating in a fully competitive market. Most of them were in fact operating as semi-monopolistic suppliers, much in the same way as they always had done, except that they were now reporting to institutional and private shareholders. Consequently most are making substantial profits.

In managing change they are at least able to take organizations like Hanson and Marks & Spencer as role models. The factory managers in the former Soviet Union trying to turn MiGs into washing machines have no such models, and are unlikely to get any until they allow Western companies like McDonalds to lead the way.

So it is in the former state-run enterprises in Britain that some of the biggest experiments in culture change are being made. The new management teams have new and impatient shareholders, and realize that 'service to the community' is a role that ceased officially when the share price was set. The sense of shock in these organizations has numbed many employees who would like to adapt but have no idea what is expected of them, apart from vague exhortations to be more productive, quality-orientated or competitive – which is difficult when you are part of a semi-monopoly.

For once the Americans have no useful experience to offer.

Internal Initiatives

Some change in organizations comes from inside, perhaps as a result of the arrival of a new chief executive or an innovative spirit. Successful organizations are more likely to be leading the changes than reacting to one of the three external pressures described above. The kind of organization in which you are working will probably indicate whether it is likely to be an **initiator** or a **follower** in the future.

How Do You Decide What Kind of Culture to Develop?

To find out what kind of culture will meet the demands of the relevant market, you need to know how things are done *now* and why people behave in the way they do.

Ingrained habits for example may be bad for business. In British Rail the planners who set the schedules epitomize the inward-looking 'task' culture. The train timetables are masterpieces of planning, making sure enough rolling stock is in place where it is needed. And yet the first train from London arrives in Manchester after two British Airways shuttles have already completed the same journey. British Rail *is* trying, but old habits die hard and tend to be defended with all kinds of user-unfriendly justification.

For organizations which decide that their habits and ways are holding them back or threatening their survival, it may be natural to express that frustration in vague exhortations about cutting costs and increasing productivity. These measures may be necessary, but to address the bad habits and change the culture, management needs some kind of process. The journey involves six steps:

1. **Recognize** the need for change.

2. **Research and understand** the ecology of your organization.

3. **Decide** what needs to change.

4. **Share** an understanding of the need for change.

5. **Work together** on the diagnosis.

6. **Start** all over again.

1. **Recognize the need for change.**
   The need for change must be endorsed by the organization's leaders. This need is often brought home to them more powerfully by comments from outsiders such as journalists,

customers or shareholders. Complacent managers may listen to an outsider more readily than an insider, and a quiet word with a journalist, a trusted analyst or a non-executive director might do the trick.

It is not disloyal to get things onto the agenda in this way. Even senior managers sometimes have trouble seeing the wood for the trees, especially if things have gone well for a long time. They need room to save face.

2. **Research and understand the ecology of your organization.**
    Research can provide that same opportunity. Good chief executives, like clever politicians, always try to make sure they are the first to know. So the next step is to understand how the organization behaves, what its role is, how it is special and what everyone's place is in it. Think about the organization as a group of co-existing tribes. The actions of one tribe directly affect another, and any inquiry should look for the key relationships which decide the behaviour and reputation of the whole.

    The research – whether it is carried out by the staff team or a consultancy – must involve employees, to make them feel they are part of something which will result in positive action. This differentiates it from much of the pollster type of research which gets no further than the chief executive's desk.

    Complete the picture by comparing the employees' view with that of the key outside groups on which the organization relies for its survival. Armed with this intelligence, which should be gathered regularly to allow the changes to be tracked, the leaders of the organization can make rational judgements about which 'habits' need to change.

3. **Decide what needs to change.**
    For the third step the organization's leaders have to ask themselves some difficult questions. What is it like to work in, or do business with the organization?

    This can be an emotionally charged process, and leaders often have to recognize that they and their predecessors have set examples, and must therefore themselves change the most.

Many excellent quality programmes have changed important things on the shop floor, only to be undermined by bickering among the 'barons' who have set no quality targets which can address the *source* of the shop floor problems.

The best and probably the only way to get time for this kind of review is to take the top layer of management away from the office. Before leaving, they can be asked to complete a brief questionnaire which will cause them to think about the organization's habits and how they affect its customers, its ability to keep key employees, and the impact on other groups which are critical to their own success. These managers are most interested in their own survival, so the review should allow them to see a personal benefit – especially if difficult changes are likely to be needed.

4. **Share an understanding of the need for change.**
A good example of a high profile campaign to raise employees' sense of pride in their organization was that of Ford's *Everything we do is driven by you* advertising initiative.

The campaign, launched on TV and posters in 1991, successfully fused Ford's corporate and quality messages. It centred on a requirement of Ford's management to see the extent to which key messages from senior management had penetrated the workforce, messages to do with the need to alter the shape of the organization in straitened times as well as those to do with quality.

Other organizations are prompted to put in place campaigns to alert employees to the need for change when they are faced with slippage in market share, manpower reduction programmes or changes in customer service requirements.

By encouraging employees to understand why the organization needs to change it is more likely that they will make the necessary changes in their attitude or in their behaviours to help the organization to meet its goals.

Some, like Ford, choose to fuse the internal and external campaigns to help employees to link their efforts to the market requirement. Other companies internalize this process to a greater extent and place greater, or sole emphasis on exhortations from senior management or direct briefings from line managers, to underscore the difference between current and desired practice.

5. **Work together on the diagnosis.**
Recognizing the need for change is, of course, only the beginning. Making the change is what counts. This part of the journey requires that senior managers not only understand the implementation process, but also accept their own part in the process.

Many management teams feel that the job is over as soon as they have decided what should happen. Nothing could be further from reality. Another common mistake is to think that all they have to do is communicate their thinking to employees. It is an understandable reaction: the work of deciding what needs to change will have been demanding and there will be a natural desire to act swiftly. But – just like the management team – all employees need to discover for themselves the rationale for change and their own part in it.

One answer is to put employees through a structured training course to help them understand the organization's competitive challenge. The course can also outline the changes that are planned, and encourage employees to work out how they can help the organization to make the shift.

Levels of hierarchy on the course should be mixed. Senior managers have tended to keep themselves aloof from the day-to-day implementation process. At the 1991 Quality Circles Convention at Warwick University, supervisors and staff felt that managers were too far removed from their place of work and spent too much time introducing impractical changes. Clearly change needs to be a joint effort. If it is dreamed up in an ivory tower, it won't work.

6. **Start all over again.**
Most management teams and staff groups talk about their exhaustion with change and 'initiatives'. Our survey of chief executives, *The Power of the Open Company*, showed that the

most consistently profitable companies avoided one-off radical reorganizations in favour of what one called a 'rolling review' of the organization's culture. The moral of their story is that if change is a routine process then everybody, management included, is more likely to be flexible.

The six step journey provides a framework for understanding what changes – if any – an organization should consider. But having a rational process is one thing, getting everybody involved in and agreeing the change – whether it is the chief executive or the driver – is quite another.

The question of how to go about managing this change is dealt with in the next chapter.

SUMMARY – MANAGING CULTURE

- Employee participation can go too far. Each organization needs to decide for itself the degree to which it is, genuinely, prepared to share power with its workforce.

- Social change, as well as market and political change, is driving changes in business.

- Management needs to think of the change process as a six step journey:

  1. **Recognize** the need for change.

  2. **Research and understand** the ecology of your organization.

  3. **Decide** what needs to change.

  4. **Share** an understanding of the need for change.

  5. **Work together** on the diagnosis.

  6. **Start** all over again.

5
Managing Change

Now everybody understands what needs to be done. But if communication begins at home, how do you set about making changes happen in an organization from the inside out?

Company boards sometimes spend hours or days debating mission statements or working out complex plans for change, expecting the rest of the staff to catch on from the contents of a hastily worded communiqué. They fail to appreciate that communication only works if people have thought through the arguments themselves.

When the government decided to encourage British Rail to make its values more commercial, the immediate reaction from staff who valued the old public service role was to reject the idea. Yet in experiments with groups of supervisors, who were asked to construct the argument themselves, for discussion with their own staff, acceptance of the new values grew in proportion to their confidence with the arguments.

Far too much emphasis has been put on one way of communicating information. However skilfully it is transmitted, it can still fail to capture people's interest. Elaborate shows and events are often organized at great cost to win people over with demonstrations of management commitment. In fact, research shows that employees usually have a healthy suspicion of glitz and glamour, and prefer straight talk and the chance of debate with supervisors and senior management.

Recognizing that employees want a face-to-face exchange is the most important starting point in planning how to communicate significant change.

But getting people involved in discovering their role requires a plan, and the following steps are vital ingredients:

1. **Communicate as part of the management process**
   A board or executive committee of the organization considering major change must think about the barriers to achieving what they want. Months of good work can be wasted if effort is not invested at the planning stage.

   Recommendations
   - Subject the implementation plan to detailed scrutiny. Quiz every aspect of the change 'plan' to make sure it is practical.

   - Make one member of the team responsible for thinking through the implementation plan. Better still, have a human resources or corporate communications professional who can play a strong role on the joint planning committee.

2. **Set up an implementation steering group**
   Many organizations set up implementation task forces, but members are often too junior to do much more than produce a list of communication techniques rather than an implementation strategy. All too often it will be expected to operate in a vacuum, separated from what one senior manager described as the 'long-trousered business of strategy'.

   Recommendations
   - Assign the board member responsible for implementation to lead the implementation steering group. Choose specialists from inside the organization, including people from the centre and devolved parts. Think about including members from outside the organization, but beware of those more interested in selling particular solutions.

- Educate the top team. Arrange a session at the beginning where a top team has to work out pragmatic criteria for testing all strategic plans as they are developed.

- Feed into the top team one or two presentations about how other organizations have managed change. It will help keep their feet on the ground.

3. Compete for employees' attention

As we saw earlier, a variety of different competing experiences go together to make up the whole experience of working for an organization.

Recommendation

- Understand the journey that your employees have to go through. Before designing an implementation process, the team should draw up a chart to help them decide the three

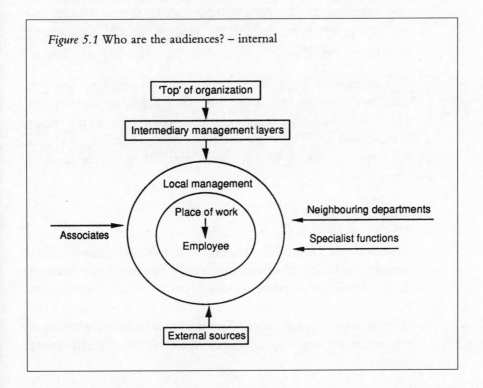

Figure 5.1 Who are the audiences? – internal

best ways of influencing their own people. You can draw on existing research, but it helps to set up a few informal focus groups with selected members of staff.

4. Communicate and involve

A great deal of the investment in house newspapers and magazines, videos, electronic mail and training is wasted, because they are not developed to suit the staff concerned. Good internal communication must be based on opportunities for debate and exchange of ideas, fed by good sources of information.

- Think about how to get everyone who is going to be affected to debate the changes. It may be that each layer of management and supervision has to plan for itself how to communicate to the people reporting to them. An existing quality programme might be a good model for getting everyone engaged.

The second challenge is to go beyond the old lazy solution of handing the 'story' over to a conference organizer and waiting for the dry ice and glitz to put the message across. Presentation skills may well provide a fun way to get the ball rolling, but they are no substitute for getting people to think through the changes for themselves.

Recommendations
- Write up the changes that the board has been considering as if it were a favourable report in a business journal. It is essential for the author to be part of the proceedings: minutes never capture the mood adequately.

- Think about how to communicate the **big picture** using all the usual outlets, including conferences, print and external media.

- Think about how to get everyone who is going to be affected to debate the changes. It may be that each layer of management and supervision has to plan for itself how to communicate to the people reporting to them. An existing quality programme might be a good model for getting everyone engaged.

- Make doubly sure that board members have been given the central parts in implementing the changes.

5. Sustain the momentum

If some of the new measures are long-term, then the implementation team should consider the following:

- Make sure the research you are planning allows you to track progress in people's attitudes. Many communication managers manage annual research programmes which allow them to compare their staff's attitudes with those of people in other organizations in their industry sector.

- Build systems of appraisal that are open and trusted. More and more organizations have introduced measures to enable employees to relate their performance to their pay. But despite the immense effort put into these programmes, very few people trust the basis for their own remuneration. But bold experiments in appraising staff by management, and vice versa, are adding to the lessons to be learnt: many organizations are now beginning to define the kind of behaviour they expect from employees and build measurable criteria into job descriptions and appraisal processes.

- Re-think the company's information systems. The ubiquitous newsletter may be adequate, but the chances are that new technology has overtaken it as the preferred source.

Are the existing systems for providing relevant information the fastest and most accurate available? If not, it is time to upgrade them.

SUMMARY – MANAGING CHANGE

- Communication can only work if people think through the arguments for themselves.

- Employees prefer straight talk and the chance of debate with senior management to glitz and glamour.

- A plan for involving people should include doing the following:

  - Communicate as part of the management process.
  - Set up an implementation steering group.
  - Compete for employees' attention.
  - Communicate by involving people.
  - Sustain the momentum.

6
Managing
External Reputation

How to become master of your own reputation by matching the external promise with the inner reality. How to do it by yourself, banishing external agencies to the status of ordinary suppliers. And how to use the Smythe Dorward Lambert 10-point Reputation Test.

We define reputation as the collective *experience* of those who work for or deal with an organization. With household items or food, the customer experience is likely to begin with its promotion, and include the shop where it is bought, its packaging and of course, whether it was any good. For more complicated products like cars, washing machines and computers, the experience will extend to after-care.

The quality of the service will depend on the quality of the people providing it, whether this is on a plane, in a bank or in the doctor's surgery.

But reputation is not confined to consumers and people on the receiving end of bureaucracies. Groups may be drawn together to raise a common voice against an organization intent on, for example, building a motorway. The protesters only have the reputation of the organization to go on before the bulldozers arrive – and that reputation can help or hinder the negotiations that follow.

Reputation also matters when big organizations make up their minds to trade or collaborate with each other. Not so long ago, North Sea oil contractors were chosen solely for their suitability for the job and their price. Today the oil majors want to be certain that contractors are accredited with a British Standards guarantee of quality. They also need to know if they are willing to operate under much tougher safety rules and will stick to minimum standards in the treatment of their workforces. The days of the cowboys are drawing to a close.

Decisions which people have to make are complex. Every member of an organization's management team needs to become more acquainted with its reputation and what can be done to modify it. This is not a job which can be left to junior managers alone.

LEARNING TO LISTEN TO CUSTOMERS

More thoughtful organizations are thinking about how to make sure their activities are relevant in the short term, but also acceptable in the long term. That means understanding that what makes money today may well come to be seen as 'disposable' when social pressure comes to bear. Firms that used to meet a real need supplying animal fur coats to keep people warm and fashionable, and which refused to see the rising tide of revulsion, are no longer in business.

The nuclear generation industry in the USA and Britain is unlikely to be a feature of modern life in a decade or two unless it can turn around its 'liar' image. This still haunts it despite the millions spent on public relations activities like plant visits for schoolchildren and local groups. The fundamental problem is that people don't trust the industry, and no amount of communication will change things until it starts to admit that it makes mistakes. This kind of change has to be made in the attitudes at the top.

Organizations are still using public relations to communicate *at* people rather than to create a dialogue which might well result in both sides changing their ways. But there are positive signs that businesses are learning to listen and accommodate the concerns of the community – and the signs are that this is paying off commercially.

One such organization is the international drinks and food conglomerate Grand Metropolitan.

'The envisaged pay-off for business is that by investing resources and developing the economic and social environment, businesses can improve the quality of the workforce, stimulate market growth and gain credibility in the community, as well as addressing social needs,' said Howard Chandler, GrandMet's Group Corporate Affairs Director.

Research from the French-backed Dragon consultancy came up with three key findings about the motivations of consumers:

- Consumers are increasingly interested in corporate reputation, and are able to evaluate corporate behaviour – but so far have little information on which to do so.

- They are willing to be favourably influenced by good corporate behaviour, but they do not expect companies just to be altruistic: they understand they are driven by commercial motives.

- They value environmental performance, employment record, community involvement, and are particularly influenced by their view of what it is like to work in the company.

One of the most vocal advocates of the need to get close to the spirit of customers is Body Shop founder Anita Roddick.

'All I want is a high profile in the community,' she says in her book *Body and Soul*. 'I'm not interested in seducing the consumer with expensive images. We've got better things to do with the money.'

HOW TO MANAGE EXTERNAL REPUTATION

Small organizations such as shops, bars and garages have to tend their local reputations with great care. There is no chance that a small business can fabricate an image which does not stand up to reality.

But then people running small businesses have the great advantage of being able to undertake on-the-spot market research, and to plan and implement radical changes without calling in a research firm, making recommendations to the board and worrying about how to get everybody to toe the line.

For this reason, the average corner store keeper could probably teach most business school professors and consultants a thing or two about managing change. They live in a world where it happens fast: when a big supermarket moves into the neighbourhood, they have to move quickly into a long hours operation which caters for people's requirements outside their big shopping trip every week.

THE CHANGING ROLE OF PR

Small businesses are either in touch and in sympathy with their customers or they are out of business. That is the way it has always been. But the ways that big business deals with the world have been changing in the last two decades, particularly in the way in which they use public relations.

● **1970s: selling, promoting and defending**
   The consumer revolution was building up in the 1970s, and the role of corporate PR was to help sell and promote the organization and its products. Although the first environmental stirrings were taking place in Europe and the USA, neither side managed much of a dialogue with the other and industry felt it needed to defend its right to produce.

   PR people were often hired from the ranks of the press for their skills with the written word. Their backgrounds confirmed that the role of PR was dealing with the press. The defensive attitudes of the organizations they worked for meant that public relations officers often had to act as barriers for people at the top. This earned the PR role a justifiably bad name as the experts in cover-up.

- **1980s: consulting and persuading**

  Corporations recognized that consulting with the various groups it was trying to persuade was better than stonewalling and failing to answer journalists' phone calls.

  It was also the decade when 'public affairs' came of age in the USA. Every organization was having to deal with a welter of environmental legislation. They turned to lobbyists to keep an eye on legislation, getting it changed or dropped by using contacts behind the scenes.

  The 1980s saw the inexorable rise of three types of external agency: the international advertising conglomerates, the world-wide PR firms and the corporate design firms. But a new environmentalism also began to emerge, and organizations were forced to question the style of their relationship with customers and the world around them.

- **1990s: predicting and negotiating**

  The 1990s may well see the identification of mutual interests as the hallmark of how progressive organizations manage their relationships with everybody who deals with them.

  'There is ample evidence that business is willingly and enthusiastically accepting a wider role in the community,' said GrandMet's Howard Chandler. 'There is also a burgeoning number of consumer protection agencies who are only too keen to advise customers and consumers about which businesses are community oriented or environmentally-friendly, before they make their purchases. So in both the US and the UK, business has a stick and carrot for its philanthropic policies.'

Even now, forward-looking organizations are having to look at their public relations functions in a totally different way. The very term 'public relations' is no longer able to encompass the role that a new breed of professional is performing.

More and more commununciation professionals are adopting titles like 'corporate communications' and 'corporate affairs' rather than public relations. The difference reflects a real change in their role. But the old style of communication is still all too common, especially in bureaucratic, hierarchical organizations where the professional communications slot will probably still be reserved for a tired manager who would otherwise be put out to grass or, worse still, the kind of ex-journalist who takes long boozy lunches.

In the diagram below, this old style of communication is represented on the right hand side. There the role is about promoting, selling, telling and explaining. It is invariably something that happens after the decisions have been made.

This attitude to communication is typical of a sales-led organization, where public relations is seen as helping the sales effort. Practical skills like managing print and promotional materials or getting 'free editorial' in the press, are prized. Public relations involvement in fashioning the message about the organization will often be limited to writing the corporate brochure or the chairman's statement in the annual report.

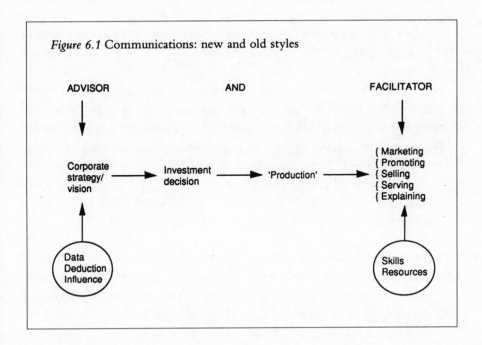

Figure 6.1 Communications: new and old styles

Contrasting with this very tactical approach are the activities on the left side of the diagram, concerned with understanding the immediate needs of employees and customers and, in the longer term, with looking to identify issues and opportunities.

The professional communicator in this situation has access to, and may well be part of, the organization's most senior management. He or she will be consulted by colleagues about the communication implications of decisions *before* they are taken.

There are two great difficulties that any new communicator faces when trying to get a more pro-active approach accepted by the management team. The first difficulty is that many managers don't understand how the reputation of the organization is created and communicated. Even if they have had management training, it is unlikely to have included a serious look at image, reputation and the role of communication. They will need some help.

The second difficulty is all the noise and flux in what communications consultant John Harben calls the 'corporate auditorium' discussed later in this chapter.

1. DEVELOPING COMMUNICATIONS IN MANAGEMENT

The first problem meant that communications management skills must be built into training for managers and supervisors – they are different from the skills needed for interpersonal communication. The key to this is exercises which require managers to 'discover' how the reputation of their organization was created and is sustained. They are then asked to deduce how their own role affects the reputation and what formal communication, marketing and human resource functions can be expected to do.

The Example of Chevron UK

The UK subsidiary of the American oil company Chevron provides a good example of how the link between communication and corporate goals can be made in managers' minds.

Cedric Lavington, Chevron's head of government and public affairs, had felt uneasy about the way that communication was seen as a specialist activity conducted by his department. He felt sure that management colleagues saw little commercial value in 'communicating'. We interviewed all the top managers individually and asked them which external audiences they had to deal with to get their own job done, and what barriers prohibited their achievement of their objectives. These audiences varied from the UK licensing authority for North Sea oil to local communities where the company operated, the media, joint venturers and, of course, their own staff.

It became clear that they were sometimes unable to provide a company stance on critical and sensitive issues, and were forced to remain silent or respond as best they could. Not only did people feel they had only half the picture, but they were at times providing different stories to staff and key outside groups.

The company decided that it needed to develop a mechanism to work out what the important issues were and produce a stance on them. This has taken the form of a panel of senior managers. They meet quarterly and review the main issues which the business has had to deal with over the previous six months and how well the communication about them was handled by the management.

These include technical issues such as deciding what position the company should take about continuing to use oil-based muds in drilling: there is an environmental argument to do away with them and the company needs to consider developing a policy and how to communicate it. The panel can forecast which issues will emerge over the next six months. These are then referred to the full management committee, where task teams are assigned to carry out the necessary work.

Every year the group tries to create a small number of big themes as an umbrella for all the on-going communication programmes. External and internal research is used to help take a decision on these.

The following diagram illustrates how the research feeds into the discussion. It also demonstrates the link that has been made between the organization's business strategy and its communication plans.

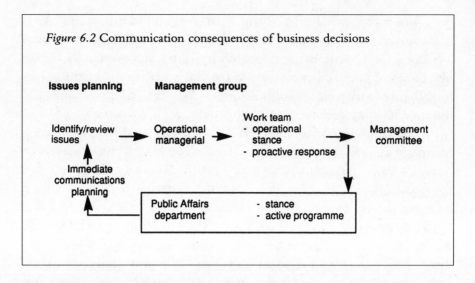

Figure 6.2 Communication consequences of business decisions

Our work at Chevron started out as a small exercise involving what some people thought was a wasteful discussion on corporate profile. It ended with the management of communications becoming a key part of the way Chevron does business.

If the subject is approached from the perspective of the individual manager's role, it is possible to get managers – even those who are hostile at first – to engage in a debate and agree new responsibilities.

2. THE CORPORATE AUDITORIUM

The second difficulty facing those concerned with managing external reputation is the constant 'noise and flux'. The bewildering pace of activity in the 1980s has made the loyalty of shareholders highly unpredictable, and tougher times have encouraged short-termism. The local communities that sustain the organization's operations can be politically and socially volatile. Trends in education and demographics make recruitment a nightmare, and staff at all levels are increasingly unlikely to stay with one organization during their working lives.

As the individual faces of staff, commentators, customers, shareholders and regulators recede into vague awareness, the script – and at times the scenery as well – are changing with such bewildering frequency that it is all the leading players can do to concentrate, let alone keep the attention of the audience.

At any time the glaring lights and hubbub of TV crews may descend – tripping from the vague awareness of the foyer in this or a hundred other corporate shows – to crash to the front and bring ten seconds of a poorly-lit scene to unknown millions. The solutions to this modern problem are suggested in Section IV.

The metaphor of the auditorium has much to teach us about learning our corporation's 'lines' and delivering them, word perfect, to the paying audience.

DO YOUR OWN REPUTATION TEST

The 10-point **Smythe Dorward Lambert Reputation Test** [TM] should be completed individually on paper or in a one-to-one interview. Try the test for yourself.

1. **Who are your customers?**
   If you work in a public service organization, such as a police force or municipal authority, then identify its users instead. Segment the customers and users into groups of people who have things in common. For example, Apple Computers' customers will vary from huge corporations to smaller businesses with a handful of PCs.

2. **What journey do they make when they deal with you?**
   For each category of customer and user, list the circumstances in which they come across the organization. It might include your promotional activity, a phone call, a meeting, a proposal, or actual consumption of your product and use of the service.

3. **What are the critical success factors?**
   Give three reasons why customers end up buying from your organization or which cause them to be content with the service.

4. **What is special about your organization's reputation?**
   Now pinpoint the invisible difference which seems to go beyond

the fulfilment of straightforward criteria like price, fitness for purpose, length of relationship and consistency of service. Make yourself articulate just one idea which makes all the difference. Respondents who have spent considerable parts of their working lives in the organization often have a breathtakingly prejudiced certainty about what makes the organization's products and services successful.

5. **Where do employees make the difference?**
Now identify where on the customer's or user's journey do the attitudes, actions and behaviours of employees – including managers – make a positive difference in their choice of your organization over its competitors.

6. **Can you describe in one or two sentences the objectives of your organization's formal communication strategy?**
This will reveal whether you share a knowledge and understanding of the communication strategy.

7. **Where and how does the effect of the formal communication strategy influence people's decision to buy, or their satisfaction with the organization?**
Depending on how well you were able to respond to Question 6, it should be possible to think about the positive influence your communication strategy has on customers.

8. **How well acquainted are you and your colleagues with:**
   - All the factors which have made – and still make – the organization commercially successful or socially relevant?

   - Your own role in giving a lead which helps other people sustain a critical edge in their attitudes and actions?

   - The research and informal processes that keep a watch on customer satisfaction?

- The connection between this research and your programmes of internal and external communication and involvement?

9. **Ask yourself whether it would be useful to compare your views with those of immediate colleagues, other employees and outsiders which influence the organization's success?**

10. **Should you:**
    - Review together as a one-off stock-taking exercise?

    - Set up a management process to keep you in closer touch with the normal course of events?

The test is designed to create an appetite for discussion of these issues. The next chapter looks at the resources needed for communication, and the relationships with complementary disciplines like marketing, human resources and personnel – and how all these need to be working together, rather than following their own often conflicting goals.

SUMMARY – MANAGING EXTERNAL REPUTATION

- All members of the organization's management team need to become more acquainted with their reputation and what can be done to change it.

- Organizations are learning to listen to and accommodate the concerns of the community – and the signs are that this is paying off commercially.

- The 1990s will see the identification of mutual interests as the hallmark of how progressive organizations manage their relationships.

- These organizations are looking at public relations in a totally different way.

- Two difficulties faced by new corporate communicators:
  - Many managers don't understand how reputation is created and communicated.
  - The noise and flux in the 'corporate auditorium'.

- The Smythe Dorward Lambert Reputation Test ™:
  1. Who are your customers?

  2. What journey do they make when they deal with you?

  3. What are the critical success factors?

  4. What is special about your organization's reputation?

  5. Where do employees make the difference?

  6. Can you describe the objectives of your organization's formal communication strategy?

7. Where and how does your formal communications strategy influence people's decision to buy, or their satisfaction with the organization?

8. How well acquainted are you with the links between research and communication?

9. Would it be useful to compare your views with those of immediate colleagues, other employees and outsiders which influence the organization's success?

10. Should you:
    – Review together as a one-off stock-taking exercise?
    – Set up a management process to keep you in closer touch with the normal course of events?

Part Three

Managing Internal Communication

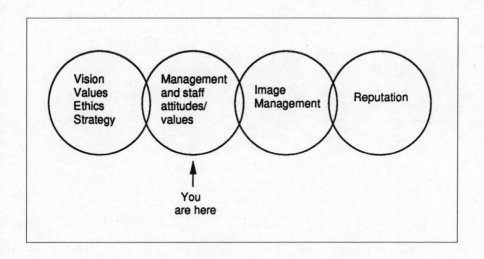

7

The Power of Internal Communication

How to set about planning a system of internal communication, without raising hopes and without confusing people. Internal communication *is* powerful, but there are three things to think about first – style, direction and focus.

As products become more similar, markets overlap and management becomes more difficult, more organizations are finding that effective internal communication gives them an untapped competitive advantage.

It differentiates their products and employment, and it does so in the service delivered by staff, in the consistency and quality of its products and in attitudes about working in the organization – all of which help attract and retain high calibre staff.

But internal communication means more than just house journals, and more even than the problem of how messages are created and targeted. It is also about the attitudes that exist across organizations: it is these which decide whether people listen to the messages they are sent and which affect the way they interpret them. We live *in* communication at work, just as we do when we are with friends and family.

Focusing on internal communication leads us onto the second circle of the Reputation Diagram (see page 59).

What people say inside the corporation and how they say it has traditionally been given less attention than convincing the public outside. Employees are after all paid to be present and to perform. Why expend more energy, time and resources on dedicating them to what ought to be their duty? The labourer should be worthy of his hire.

But a growing number of corporations, large and small, have recognized the links between how productive and how satisfied their workers are.

Organizations like Marks & Spencer and Cadbury are proud of their staff communications and all-encompassing welfare activities. The long period over which they have enjoyed these reputations and their distinctive positions in their markets, are largely because of the effort put into communicating with their workforces. They have instilled in them a commitment to a corporate mission and the values that lie behind it. They have created sustainable reputations for themselves, with realistic expectations and an awareness of their social contribution. Together these give them added value among consumers and investment communities.

Greater access to information is fuelling people's expectations of information about their work and its future. Increasingly sophisticated information systems – home computers, satellite television and high quality 'life-style' magazines – are encouraging them to want better sources of information at work.

The best corporations have recognized this, so the management of internal communication is becoming more important in the portfolio of management techniques. There are three key dimensions to this: style, focus and direction.

STYLE

People experience internal communication in different ways. If the goal is a compliant workforce that knows what it needs to know, then internal communications are likely to provide only the detail they need in order to do what is expected of them. This 'style' of communication is known as **instructional**.

If the goal is to help the workpeople to understand what they are doing, why they are doing it and how it relates to the organization's objectives, then there is a need to 'inform' as well as to instruct. This style is **informative**. It is also a one-way process. The information that is thought suitable is identified at the top of the organization and is broadcast downwards. Being informative is not about providing opportunity for debate. It is about delivering messages.

The third style of internal communication, the **consultative** style, provides for interaction. It recognizes that people will be more receptive to the messages they are given if they can be involved in debate and consultation in the course of their delivery. This allows the message to be clarified and gives an opportunity for staff to feel confident that their views have been sought and their concerns respected. It makes communication less impersonal – with fewer rules, dictates and procedures.

The consultative style provides a basis for making an organization more effective, but it puts demands onto managers who have not necessarily been trained for it or selected for their ability to adopt it as part of their management style.

Involving is our fourth communication style. It recognizes that staff represent a reservoir of informed observation about improvements and it tries to tap that source of expertise. This gives employees the opportunity to share their own experiences at work. It recognizes that today's workforces are demanding more of their employers but that, if they are treated well, they are prepared to give more effort and add more value than they may have before. Involvement reverses the traditional communication process. It seeks the views of junior staff to shape the decisions of senior staff.

Consultation is two-way whereas involvement is both bottom up and two-way. Consultation requires communication skills, involvement requires management skills. A **participative** style is the fifth in our hierarchy of communication, and goes still further. It *guarantees* that the voice of workers is heard and acted upon.

An involving style respects the opinions of staff, but does not give a guarantee of action. Participation does. It is practised in many European countries throught the mechanics of Worker Representative Councils, and allows employees to voice their opinion of management plans and to recommend alterations to proposals – which management is then obliged to think about and act on.

Our five styles of internal communication represent a hierarchy. It is easier to instruct than it is to inform, and to inform than it is to consult, but effective instruction and information is a necessary foundation for constructive consultation and involvement or participation.

The Example of The Royal Mail
In order to create a shared understanding about the objectives of communication programmes, choosing the right style is vital.

In 1989, Britain's Royal Mail Letters tried to improve communication in its workforce by refining an existing team briefing process. Managers met their staff regularly to pass on core messages that had cascaded down through the structure, as well as to relay local information. But whereas management saw the team briefing as information dissemination, the staff saw it as a consultation which was aimed at involving them. The confusion led to conflict with the trade unions, communication blocks, legal action and eventually – and inevitably – a loss of credibility for team briefing inside the Royal Mail.

The reason team briefing failed in the Royal Mail when it was first introduced was because of the confusion about what it was trying to achieve. The organization was not yet ready to launch a consultative communication approach. Staff were used to getting the real stuff from their unions and managers felt uncomfortable communicating information which they themselves did not fully understand, and they quickly viewed the team briefing process as ineffective.

The Example of the Milk Marketing Board
Consultative staff communication and increasing the involvement of employees is a distant target for many organizations. It is not necessarily the first port of call. Information has to be flowing easily beforehand.

These conditions are unlikely to be present during periods of crisis or deep instability. Early in 1990, Britain's Milk Marketing Board was trying to create a greater sense of involvement for its workforce. The board knew that there was a great deal of anxiety and wanted at least to dilute it. The cause of the anxiety was that people were uncertain about the future of the organization and their job security.

What the Milk Marketing Board needed in the short term was *not* a staff involvement process, but some clear messages about the options they faced from an authoritative source, and the reasons and implications of them. Not all organizations can improve their lot by encouraging staff involvement: they must have the right understanding among staff and management to support an approach like that. If a demanding communication process is introduced too early, this can kill it off for decades.

This is why, as we will see later, the first requirement is a period of purposeful investigation.

DIRECTION

Should communications be top down, bottom up or lateral? Most communication in most organizations is predominantly characterized by top down messages from key points in the organization that are broadcast down the hierarchy. Some of these may be direct and face to face – like team briefings or departmental meetings. Others may be indirect, such as newsletters, memos and notices.

Getting the direction right means acknowledging that there are three centres of interest: the centre or corporate headquarters, the other sites or locations where people work and the tightly-knit groups which form the daily work team. The organization's communications need to look after all of these.

Bottom up Communication
Bottom up communication means finding out views and ideas from staff throughout the organization to provide information for senior managers and a sense of involvement for junior staff. Techniques include suggestion schemes, quality circles, staff question-and-

answer sessions and round table lunches with the chief executive.

Three questions arise:

- How purposeful can these consultations be?

- How useful is it really for those at the top to have a reservoir of intelligence and a bank of unanswered questions from junior staff?

- Is it really possible to create a sense of involvement among staff by asking them to participate in suggestion schemes?

- The answers are probably: Not much, Not much and No.

'It was totally useless,' said one client about the suggestion scheme in her organization. 'In the first six months we got 5,000 suggestions, most of which were not feasible and anyway we couldn't deal with the volume.'

Communication works best when people's attention is engaged on issues that are most relevant to them. This generally means issues of a local, and frequently parochial concern. Bottom up communication tends to work best when it involves groups of staff in a debate about their own place of work or area of activity. Similarly, top down communications are better received when their point of origin is closer to the person receiving it.

One large British company recently split its activities into five distinct business areas, each operating as a separate commercial entity, but remaining part of the corporate holding company. Despite the fact that the organization had encouraged its managers to run their own profit centres it still felt a desire to communicate directly with all of its staff.

So a system of cascade communications called Chief Executive's Briefing was established. Superbly produced packs of professionally presented information were created and distributed throughout all the newly created profit centres for managers to cascade to all staff. But their delivery was frustrated as the materials passed through the organization. Junior staff had little interest, and certainly little understanding, of the complex financial and business messages from the rather distant centre of the organization. They were more interested in the briefings that came from inside their own business areas. And they were even more interested in briefings about their own local site, such as team discussions about their own production line or departmental activities.

Far from opening up communications in the company, as it was designed to do, the Chief Executive's Briefing system fuelled irritation among staff and management alike and discredited the idea of establishing a series of connected but independent profit centres.

The Example of Tootal
Far more workable was the approach to communication adopted by the UK textile manufacturer Tootal, before it merged with Coats Viyella in 1991. Tootal encouraged local managers to concentrate on improving staff communication at the local level. This meant that different approaches to staff communication existed in different parts of the group, but still each one was thought appropriate by the people who had to make them work. They were more heavily supported and promoted by local senior management than would have been the case if the various initiatives had been designed and managed from group headquarters.

The Example of Post Office Counters
The Post Office split itself into four operating companies in 1986. Communication inside Post Office Counters was hampered by a series of factors including a cultural heritage of militaristic, bureaucratic communication. Staff were worried about their futures, and there was speculation about the reduction of Crown Post Office outlets and continuing rumours of privatization. Post Office Counters had gone a long way towards instilling a sense of customer service amongst its more than 100,000 staff and agents, but was still finding customer service falling below desired target levels.

What had been overlooked was how many barriers had been built up between the head office departments. The sequence of operations needed for paper-based transactions over the counter in most offices around the country were also extremely varied and complex. Few people in the organization knew enough about the internal processes of which they were part – and therefore how their work affected other people further down the processing track. The importance of the external customer had been trumpeted loud and clear, but there had been little regard for the internal customer.

By improving communication between these primary operating departments at head office and area offices, and by creating a better understanding among staff of how they fitted into the family of transactions, internal communication improved. Ultimately the external customer would receive a quicker and more reliable service.

FOCUS

This is about the source of the message that needs to be communicated. Different audiences within the organization will react in different ways to messages originating from different sources.

They will view a message from their immediate line manager differently from one they think has originated in the chief executive's office – even if it is the same message, communicated by the same person. The credibility of the message depends on how much the department it came from is respected.

One large manufacturing company, under threat from a hostile takeover, established a very effective communication system in which the chief executive faxed all their locations around the world every day. Only a small number of faxes were actually delivered – perhaps five per location – but photocopies of the fax were widely circulated very quickly. The situation demanded rapid and credible messages from an authoritative source. Technology provided the speed; the chief executive provided the credibility. Had the same messages been delivered by each managing director of each operating company, or by the corporate communications department, it is unlikely that they would have been awarded the same degree of urgency.

The five 'styles' of communication are important if you are designing a complete communication infrastructure, but the effect of 'focus' is useful if messages are to have a specific effect.

SUMMARY – THE POWER OF INTERNAL COMMUNICATION

- Attitudes across organizations determine how much people listen to the messages sent in their direction.

- Corporations are beginning to recognize the links between the satisfaction of their employees and their productivity.

- There are three dimensions to resolving communication problems:
    - Style: instructional, informative, consultative, involving or participative.
    - Direction: top down communications are better received when their point of origin is closer to the person receiving them.
    - Focus: the credibility of the message depends on how much the department from which it came is respected.

8
The Human Dimension

How to prepare the ground by improving the communication skills of the people in the organization, and why training alone is not enough to give you effective communications. A plan for creating a communication ethos.

Most organizations invest large amounts of time and money training their staff in communication. Some courses are designed for senior management to improve their presentation skills; others are designed for first line supervisors to help them communicate verbally with their immediate work teams.

These courses are useful, even if all they do is provide people with a focus. But despite the magnitude of their effort, most organizations remain disappointed with the result.

Team briefing – a cascade process which passes information down the line – relies on managers at all levels of the hierarchy to pass on the messages. It often falters because of the inability of the people to communicate verbally with confidence in front of groups – even if they are their own staff.

The Example of Royal Mail Letters

One of the causes of the failure of team briefing in Royal Mail Letters, for example, was that supervisors were not confident about having to communicate formally with their teams.

Many of the staff were frustrated at attending what they thought were valueless briefing sessions because managers were not able to communicate adequately. They wanted a team of professional communicators to be responsible for conducting the sessions throughout the business. In this way, the staff argued, not only would they get well-communicated messages, but the organization would also be guaranteed a consistent delivery of the message.

Many of the managers were keen on this approach too. Preparing a presentation and communicating with their staff was something they were not used to and did not expect to be asked to do. Many felt uncomfortable playing the role of communicator instead of their usual role of inspector. They particularly disliked being responsible for messages from senior management which they did not fully understand and sometimes did not agree with.

But the solution of professionally trained, dedicated briefers was ruled out. It was exactly the opposite of what Royal Mail Letters was trying to achieve – coherence, identity and liaison between working teams and their immediate managers. It received such widespread support because of the anxiety communication can put on staff, which is exactly why well-designed and well-executed communication skills training programmes are so important.

TRAINING IS NOT ENOUGH

But training alone will not provide the organization with effective communication. It will not resolve the organizational difficulties, many of which are likely to have been a problem for some time. These can get in the way of effective communication, and might include the structure of the organization, the structure of the communication network, the balance of power between the centre of the organization and its parts – even evaluation processes that fail to value interpersonal skills.

The training needs to be reinforced with regular refresher

courses, and the philosophical component – the message that explains why the skill needs to be learnt – must be backed by a visible commitment from the holders of power in the organization and given proper resources.

Organizations can easily fall into the trap of providing training and forgetting all the other factors that need to be resolved if it is to generate the desired effect.

MAKING COMMUNICATION A CORE VALUE

The organization needs constantly to reinforce the message that communication is a vital pulse within the business. It is not a process – it is not only a criteria of performance – it is a philosophy that is integral to the way people think about their work. Even bad communicators will then do more to improve and promote their communication abilities. Good communicators will realize that their communication track record is a measure of their ability as managers and an important way they can progress in their career. In an environment like that, they will shine.

Providing a wealth of training courses does not absolve senior management from directing and guiding the organization's conscience so that communication is respected as a necessary management focus. Everyone has to understand the importance that is attached by the business to good internal communication, particularly among teams that work together and between managers and supervisors and their immediate staff groups. The best time to create this understanding is when new recruits, at whatever level, join the organization.

MAKING THE JOINING EXPERIENCE EFFECTIVE

The joining experience is more than just induction: it also extends back through the recruitment process. It should screen out people who might have the right mix of skills or balance of experience, but whose outlook does not fit with the ethos of the organization and the values it holds dear.

Potential employees should be told about the importance that the organization gives to internal communication before they are offered the job. They should be asked for commitment to this and other values that the organization believes to be important as part of the 'deal' when joining the organization.

Commitment will be easier to win at this time than at any other during the individual's employment in the organization, because at this stage both sides expect a deal to be struck.

Establishing this commitment means that both the recruitment and the induction experience need to:

- Set down the values that the organization believes to be important in guiding behaviour. Say what these are in recruitment literature and back them up with anecdotes in which they can be seen to have had an impact on decisions or operations. Get each applicant to read them through before or during an interview and use them as a basis for discussion during the interview. Ask each applicant if he or she agrees with the principles and would be comfortable working in an environment that supports that type of approach.

    Make sure you provide enough opportunities during the induction process for the values to be explained and for people to find out what they imply in practice. That means treating new recruits in a manner consistent with those values and providing real or imaginary work situations for them to experience.

- Explain how the organization works and how its various parts fit together. This can be achieved with carefully planned experiences of working in different departments for relatively short periods of time, by providing new employees with formal tuition about the organization they are joining, and by supporting all this 'education' with a package of relevant internal and market literature.

    You can supplement this with occasional 'exchange' visits of staff between key operating areas that frequently interact with each other. Many insurance companies, for example, provide opportunities for staff from head office to work for short periods of time in area offices, and vice versa, so that everyone understands the pressures that the other is under.

- Clarify the role of the individual being recruited or inducted in the organization. Many organizations make use of videos or audio tapes for this. They usually contain messages of welcome from the chief executive and other key figures, which express the vision, values and mission of the organization and explain the role of each individual in achieving them.

- Show the value to the consumer – internal and external – and to society of the product or service to which the individual will be contributing.

ENCOURAGING PEOPLE TO BE GOOD COMMUNICATORS

Everyone in the management hierarchy needs to recognize the role they have to play in making communication work. They must also understand their responsibility to make it work, that they are accountable for good communications in their own area, and that their performance will be evaluated on their contribution to communication as much as the contribution to finance.

Some organizations are now recognizing the link between effective internal communication, external reputation and sales. One major UK corporation is experimenting with a new bonus scheme that links all payments to a general level of customer satisfaction. It measures service to customers by comparing it with those of its competitors, by looking at a client's particular 'account', and at service actually delivered in the field.

Each of these measurements forms a key part of evaluating performance. It also provides the basis for recognizing individual areas for improvement and effort, and contributes to the general level of overall bonus awards paid out to every employee on an equal basis.

In other organizations that measure people's individual perform-ance as communicators, managers are finding that more attention is being paid to staff communication, and the communication responsibilities detailed in job descriptions are being respected and acted on. This means that the link between internal communication and profits is being recognized.

INVOLVING EVERYBODY WITH A MISSION STATEMENT

Britain's current craze for 'customer charters' is making many public sector organizations rethink their attitudes to communication in the race to improve the quality of their service to the public. As well as producing these charters for people who use their services they are also – like their colleagues in the private sector – experimenting with 'communications charters' as a way of informing and involving staff in the organization.

Many large, traditional organizations also find that reviewing and relaxing their rules for classifying information as 'confidential' goes a long way to opening the mouths and ears of staff and managers.

But this is ultimately little more than a gesture. Getting people to recognize their role means getting them to discuss how better communication will help them fulfil their objectives and contribute to the organization's mission.

A corporation needs a mission statement to the extent that it can serve to encapsulate why it exists and what it is trying to achieve. It provides a sense of direction and a clear focus for initiative and action. From a mission statement come objectives, and these are milestones towards achieving the mission. So the mission statement has a powerful role to play.

Ideally, the statement is the core philosophy on which everything else is built. It reflects the source of value that the organization provides to society and the basis of motivation that encourages staff effort.

Organizing Group Discussions
Once you have an appropriate mission statement effectively communicated, you need a foundation on which to discuss the role of

communication if the team is going to be successful. This foundation is frequently built up by using the information gained from – for example – an employee attitude survey (see Chapter 10) as the basis for a range of developmental seminars around the organization. These can involve relevant groups of managers or of managers and their staff. The audit's findings can be played back and used as the basis of various team-based exercises to illustrate the role that communication must play if some of the difficulties exposed by the survey are to be overcome.

These debates are easier to manage if the participants are disciplined to focus their thinking on the areas under review. We have created these forms for sessions with management teams in several of our client companies. (Figure 8.1)

Many organizations have found this technique powerful and effective. Powerful because, often for the first time, it forces individuals to think and work together as teams which may have existed conceptually or by design – but did not work in practice. Effective because the exercises help to break down barriers, expose prejudices or misconceptions and enable people to respect the fact that each has valid views and constructive comments to contribute. The experience also bonds the team, and provides an opportunity to help people realize their own role in the communication process.

Creating Communication Action Plans

In practice, all this talking has only short-term value if it does not lead to agreed actions and become enshrined in new codes of behaviour. So it is important that the participants agree to create 'Communication Action Plans'. These are the blueprints outlining what managers intend to do in every part of the business structure. They should not consist of grandiose statements of strategic intent from the centre. Their job is to establish standards, guidelines and expectations about the conduct of local managers with their staff.

The plans should identify responsibilities and define how managers will communicate with their teams. They should also underline the importance of listening, providing feedback and creating opportunities for consultation and debate with staff.

Individual plans from every part of the organization can then be

Figure 8.1

Current communication activity

Current briefing methods/media	Recipients	Business purpose	Strengths/ weaknesses

Work sheet 1

*Top **two** most important issues for **your** staff in the past 6 months*

What were they	How did you hear about them	How did staff hear about them

Work sheet 2

*What are the three most critical areas for development in **each** of the following?*

Understanding/ accommodating staffs' differing communication needs	Staff feedback, discussion processes	Communicating relevant information	Managing these processes
Rank	Rank	Rank	Rank

Work sheet 3

put together into an overall communication plan to be reviewed with senior management. In this way communication becomes a 'bottom up' planning process in which all the relevant managers have been engaged and for which they can all feel a sense of responsibility.

SUMMARY – THE HUMAN DIMENSION

- Training alone will not provide the organization with effective communication systems.

- Communication skills need to be reinforced with regular refresher courses and a visible commitment from the power holders.

- Communication criteria must be built into the recruitment and selection procedures.

- The best time to create an understanding about the importance of internal communication is when new recruits are joining the organization.

- Everyone in the management hierarchy needs to recognize the role they have to play in making internal communication work.

- You can make one relationship between internal communication and sales overt by linking it to the system of bonus payments.

- A mission statement should articulate the core philosophy on which everything else is built.

- Communication action plans can provide a bottom up planning process which everyone is engaged in and feels responsible for.

9
The
Organizational
Dimension

Structure *is* strategy. How to prepare the ground by improving
the structure of the organization, so that it encourages, rather
than obstructs, good communication.

The output of an organization is a result of the combined creative
input of everyone in it, of all the interactions between its different
parts, all the inefficiencies and all the positive energy that is generated
– either from determined effort or compliant action.

Maximization of corporate value means that all of these
complicated variables have to be effectively managed. Each one
needs to be managed individually, but also as part of the overall
process. They must be managed as a dynamic system which is
continuously evolving, where a change in any one factor has a
knock-on effect on all the others.

This means that effective management is about managing the co-
ordination of initiatives across departments as well as the efficient
completion of activity within functional areas.

Communication is the binding force that allows all the energies and skills throughout the organization to be brought together into a coherent whole – which makes it perhaps the most powerful source of added value that organizations have.

The most successful senior managers not only review the strategic direction of their organization constantly, they also manage it in a *questioning* way. Existing structures and systems are not accepted as given, ideal or impossible to change – even if they are providing excellent value at present. They don't subscribe to the premise 'if it ain't broke, don't fix it'. Flexibility and adaptability are recognized as prerequisites for continuing success. For these to be feasible, the organization must be continuously evolving – never standing still.

Continuous fine-tuning of an organization means that you have to understand the prevailing structures and the effect they are having on the organization's ability to perform. The more accurately they are understood, the more appropriate an approach towards communication can be designed. For this reason, good communication requires:

- A perceptive understanding of the organization's nuances.

- A clear view of how much each component needs support from other parts of the organization.

- Clear understanding inside the organization about which parts are playing a leading role in specific activities.

- Clarity about how much the centre or local operating parts are influencing daily strategic decisions.

- Understanding of the different styles of management and work environments in the organization.

- Understanding relationships between managers and staff.

This type of intelligence comes from repeated internal research to measure changes or shifts in attitudes. We will be looking at this in more detail in Chapter 10, including the importance of feedback in its use as a tool for change.

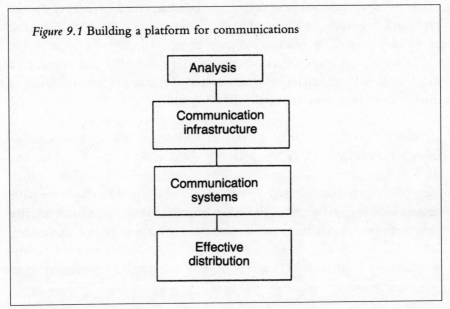

Figure 9.1 Building a platform for communications

The structure of organizations has to make it possible to get the right messages to the right people. It is not possible to separate the problem of delivering these messages from the communication itself. Once that box of beautifully produced house journals has left the central office, the corporate communicators often believe their job is done. It is not. The design of effective distribution and delivery systems is just as important as the communication media themselves. What is the point of having the perfect in-house magazine if nobody sees it, or a superb video designed for senior management which junior staff complain is too long, boring or difficult to understand?

One corporation distributed a large quantity of in-house newsletters to a divisional office, and a few weeks later the divisional manager called the communication manager and asked him where his newsletters had got to. 'I sent them to you weeks ago,' was the confident reply.

It transpired that the box of newsletters had been left lying at the bottom of a flight of stairs alongside the divisional director's office. Staff passing the box had noticed the newsletter and had taken the first few copies. As the box emptied it resembled a temporary rubbish bin, which it then became. Hundreds of copies of the expensively-produced newsletter had been covered by empty drinks cans and cigarette packets. The divisional manager had passed it every day, probably adding his own litter.

If the organization has interest groups which need to receive information from different sources for different reasons, effective distribution becomes especially important.

MATCHING MEDIA TO MESSAGE

Many organizations find it useful to undertake a periodic review to determine the efficiency of their distribution systems and the penetration of individual communication media in terms of:

- Activity: all media and methods currently employed e.g. publications, briefings, events.

- Message: the messages that the organization is trying to convey, from day-to-day operational information to strategic plans.

- Audience: relevant internal sub-divisions e.g. by location, function or grade.

against a series of criteria: purpose, content, speed and distribution itself. Try the following four-point test.

1. *Purpose*

- What is the stated purpose of the activity?
  Are the objectives explicit?

- At whom is it aimed? (Both the primary and secondary audiences.)

- Whom does it regularly reach/involve? (Remember to include both internal and external recipients.)

- With what frequency?

2. Content

- Is it designed to be one-way or two-way?

- What type of information does it contain?

  - Instructions (to do the job/follow procedures).
  - News.
  - Contextual information (e.g. about other functional departments).
  - Strategic information.

- What other messages are conveyed (e.g. via style/design/tone)?

3. Speed

- What is the expected time frame for delivery (i.e. when should the recipient get the information; at what point will it be out of date)?

- Does it meet this time scale?

- Is it a mechanism for

  - urgent news
  - time specific information/feedback

  or is there no specific time scale?

- What time lags exist between the point of distribution and the point of receipt among the various (internal and external) audiences?

- Typically how should/does it fit into the recipient's work calendar (e.g. planning period, decision-making time, information gathering stages)?

4. Distribution

- Whom does it reach? When?

- How is distribution organized (e.g. how are mailing/invitation lists updated; what delivery mechanisms are used)?

- What other audiences get to read or see it and to what extent is it possible or desirable to control this onward distribution?

- Typically, in what context is it received?

MAKING COMMUNICATION THE 'CORPORATE GLUE'

Communication is the management of the intangible – a white space or an invisible force capable of adding power and colour and *difference* to the organization. The process involves co-ordinating all the different stories that people tell, all the millions of transactions that go on every minute.

But the power of communication is not necessarily in its uniformity: it can be powerful when it is diverse. Research frequently indicates that different parts of the organization have completely different cultures. As one corporate leader said: 'It's the motivation of the sub-cultures that generates the income.' To this extent, managing communication is about creating an allegiance to the centre: an allegiance that might be expressed through different – not wrong, but different – managerial and working styles through-out the operation.

For example, if the corporation is to have a uniform identity it will require allegiance from its employees wherever they work. It needs consistency in standards, procedures and expectations. But this is different from a corporation with a devolved identity, where senior managers at the centre will probably be trying to establish *control* to avoid unilateral declarations of independence.

As if the issues of identity and allegiance were not enough, today's corporate cultures are increasingly having to cope with demands for flexibility and responsiveness. These currently popular management ideas suggest that wherever possible, decisions should be made locally, closer to the customer. This widespread develop-ment has the potential to threaten allegiance to the core identity and makes centralized management difficult.

The key to resolving these issues is to decide the role of the centre and its relationship with other parts of the organization. Communi-cation has to find and maintain the right balance between them.

WHAT KIND OF BALANCE?

But what is the balance of forces which *does* serve the organization best?

If we want an organization where policies are laid down at the centre, where compliance is rewarded and different procedures discouraged, communication is relatively easy to manage. We create a dominant visual identity and demand consistent allegiance to the centre, from where activities are managed through clearly defined rules and procedures. Communication becomes a centrally managed activity and in this situation the 'corporate communicator' will have a relatively large power base which creates the messages and sends them out.

This kind of approach was popular in the highly centralized management structures and hierarchies of the 1970s. Today, senior managers are discovering that it no longer does what they want it to do. Briefing systems based on core corporate messages are irrelevant to most who take part in them. Centrally managed communications take away from the sense of local independence which is vital for todays' rapid decisions. Even central identities are being challenged as different parts of the organization demand visible acknowledgement of their contribution to the group – either with a local identity for their part of the operation, or by downgrading the corporate logo so that it endorses a more powerful corporate sub-brand.

But as organizations become more complex, the communications task becomes more demanding and more sophisticated. Different 'sub-cultures' require different approaches. Rules are out, guidelines are in. Allegiance is hoped for but not expected. Dominant corporate cultures meet with resistance and even sabotage unless they have been an intrinsic part of the division's identity since its early development. (Figure 9.2)

The balance needed is not so much between local and central control, but between what those at the centre believe is best for the organization and what those in its parts will accept. Sometimes the two converge; sometimes they do not.

If communication is the corporate glue, it must provide the

common links in organizations that become more disparate as more sub-cultures emerge. These are likely to develop across geographic, functional or product boundaries as groups become more confident about their own ways of doing things.

One large chemical organization, with a selling operation as well as an engineering operation, has two cultures in these divisions which are entirely different. One is entrepreneurial and fast-moving, the other scientific and exactingly precise. Their differences may bring them into apparent conflict, but the corporation needs their differences – like the grit in the oyster – to bring a better product to the market.

Perhaps the most obvious cultural divides are those between national boundaries. The current attempt to create a united Europe may be the most demanding test ever of bridge-building across national divides. On a smaller scale, there is the international mining company operating across Africa, where the drive for national independence and suspicion of Western colonization requires arms' length management from the London centre. Or there is the example of the American product and service companies strengthening their European base, and having to come to terms with the fact that all countries in Europe do not speak their language – both literally and metaphorically.

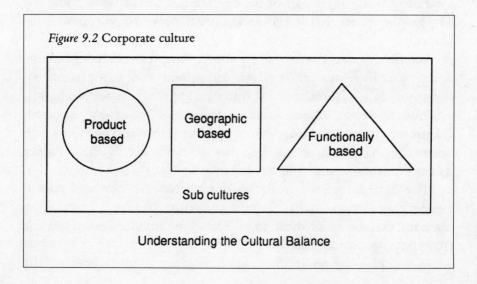

Figure 9.2 Corporate culture

Sub-cultures exist in most, if not all, organizations. Making the glue stick means recognizing and respecting that the differences need to exist. It is no longer possible to subjugate them with corporate gloss or to undermine them by posting expatriates to manage the outposts, with a job spec. resembling that of a nineteenth century district commissioner.

OVERCOMING THE PROBLEMS

The management of difference requires:

- Creating a senior management team.

- Establishing a core set of corporate values.

- Developing guidelines rather than rules.

Creating a Senior Management Team
The more the senior management act and work as a team, the easier it will be to accommodate differences of approach and to keep them together. But in order to act as a team, the top managers need to:

- Understand the different activities taking place across the group, but all within the context of a shared vision and sense of direction, and

- Respect that different approaches to dealing with issues will be adopted by senior colleagues.

Debate, argument and constructive conflict are the stuff of good decisions. Nothing is as boring or indecisive as the political conference where all delegates agree with one another. It is the same in the boardroom or at the executive management conference.

Building a good senior management team should include periodic meetings to review the state of the organization, to re-affirm the vision, mission and objectives and create workable action plans. The competitive tensions from different sub-cultures can be channel-led into a force of positive, constructive energy.

Establishing a Core Set of Values
It is the guidance and support – financial and advisory – which the centre provides which adds commercial value. It also protects the constituent parts from financial predators or political upheaval, as well as offering career planning and help for the development of skills.

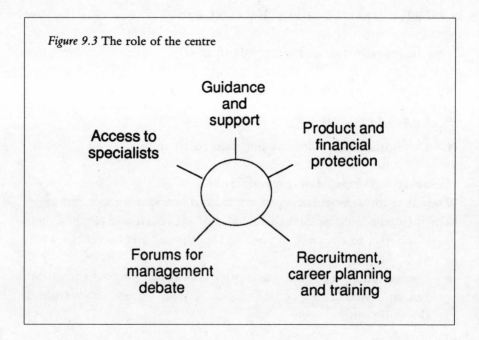

Figure 9.3 The role of the centre

Unlike a single culture across the organization, a single set of values can fit in well with all the different parts. Values describe the type of behaviour that the organization wants to promote, even though the interpretation of those values will be different in the different parts of the organization. They provide a consistent reference point.

Developing Guidelines rather than Rules
Sub-cultures, by their very nature, are unlikely to be positive about intervention in their affairs by the centre. People tend to be motivated by actions which they determine for themselves, having

weighed up the alternatives and consequences, rather than obeying instructions from a distant and perhaps invisible master.

For this reason, organizations are finding that any uniformity and standardization they want is best achieved by creating guidelines that set standards and expectations. The guidelines may recommend procedures – even set requirements – but leave room for flexibility, interpretation and individualism.

Why is this relevant in a book about communication? Because operational instructions are a key communication activity. Rules leave little room for involvement and suggest a regime of bureaucracy and control: this hardly encourages the ingenuity and motivation that drive people to work harder, longer and better. Guidelines encourage creative solutions within well-understood standards. They build a sense of ownership and appreciation at local level, and enable internal competition to be diluted by an appreciation of the value of different styles in different cultures.

Guidelines enable employees to accept, understand and work towards common objectives in a way which is real to them, so that the objectives become their *own*.

SUMMARY – THE ORGANIZATIONAL DIMENSION

- Communication is the binding force that allows all the energies and skills in an organization to be brought together into a coherent whole – and to create an allegiance to the centre.

- The most successful senior managers manage the strategic direction of their organization in a constantly *questioning* fashion.

- The design of effective distribution and delivery systems is just as important as the communication media themselves.

- The management of difference requires:
  - The creation of a senior management team.
  - The establishment of a core set of corporate values.
  - The development of guidelines rather than rules.

- Competitive tensions from different sub-cultures can be channelled into a force of positive, constructive energy.

- Guidelines enable employees to accept, understand and work towards common objectives.

10
Building the Case

Why is it that the goalposts for internal communication are always shifting? How to measure good communication in your organization, and make sure it leads to real business improvements.

Managing internal communication effectively is not a simple affair. Just when you think you've got it right, you discover a pocket of discontent, because as people experience improvements they continue to demand even more.

So what measurements can be applied? Some are definite: based on evidence of actual achievements, including determining:

- How popular are the methods used to communicate with employees?

- How relevant are the messages?

- How much are key messages remembered by people throughout the organization?

Other measurements are judgemental:

- How do people feel about their work?

- What do they think about their managers' skills as communicators?

- Do they believe in or adhere to the organization's goals and values?

These three judgemental areas are open to different interpretations, expectations and personal standards. They can only be determined by qualitative techniques – asking and listening to people's views. That does not mean that qualitative judgements have no value: quite the reverse. But it is only by combining factual and personal data that you can get an accurate measurement of success.

FINDING MEASURES OF SUCCESS

Most organizations only develop new products or marketing strategies, or invest millions in advertising campaigns, after extensive surveys into consumer reactions. More of them are now applying the same approach before committing themselves to improving internal communication, because of a recognized need to maximize the value of the investment in internal communications. A communication audit is the best way of evaluating how successfully your organization is communicating with its staff.

The audit can be designed to test success on any of the three dimensions discussed earlier:

- Style, focus and direction.

- The human dimension.

- The organizational dimension.

If you want to understand the state of your organization's communications, you need an evaluation exercise that can cover all three. Audits that concentrate on just one dimension, for example by concentrating on style and direction of communications, will not provide the understanding that you need.

In fact, the data they generate could actually be misleading. The results of the survey might indicate that the house magazine is not achieving its original intent. This could lead to a decision to stop publishing it, or to invest in it to guarantee its success. Such an audit may mask the real reason why the house magazine is not being received positively which may have little to do with its content, style, presentation, or method of delivery.

People's appreciation of any communication medium is heavily influenced by their relationships with their colleagues, their manager and with their perceptions of the whole of the organization. If employees are frustrated by the lack of open and shared dialogue with shop floor supervisors, for example, they are not going to find the house journal – necessarily a broad picture and largely one-sided – any sort of substitute. Their dissatisfaction is with the 'human dimension', not with the house journal itself.

Attitude surveys can be agents of change in themselves, but they are only the start of the process – not the full journey. Surveys that start when questionnaires are distributed and finish when a report is delivered to senior management are never likely to achieve much.

Right thinking organizations usually commission research for two reasons. First to get an accurate map of attitudes and behaviours, allegiances and motivations, which can be the basis for developing a better-targeted approach for communication. Second, to act as a catalyst for change: to engage the organization in debate and to set the agenda for improvements that will follow, so that they will be seen and accepted.

STRUCTURING THE APPROACH

There is little point in undertaking an audit unless you are committed to doing something about the results. The audit itself will raise expectations among staff that improvements are about to happen. They will think 'it's about time, but at least they're going to do something about it now'. Yet all too often staff hear little feedback from the survey and experience little change or improvement as a result of it. Usually this is because:

- The results are considered so damning that management decides not to release them.

- The senior management team disagrees about what to do next.

- The survey's credibility is in doubt because of the methodology, the sampling or the accuracy of the analysis.

These problems point to a simple fact: going around the organization asking questions of employees – either in focus groups or by questionnaire – is not a difficult task. The difficulties arise from:

- Deciding the objectives of the exercise and therefore what questions to ask.

- Deciding who to ask.

- Accommodating the different views held by senior managers about the sample and the questions.

- Managing the reaction of senior executives whose areas of responsibility come under scrutiny in the course of the survey.

The more you are able to anticipate the conflicts that the audit may generate, the more you will be able to build in processes which make it difficult for senior managers to discredit the results later on. The secret of success is, as a first step, to get the whole issue of better internal communication onto the management agenda in the form of a debate in the executive committee or its equivalent.

The result of the debate should be a clear licence to complete a more extensive audit that is likely to have a powerful impact on the entire organization.

Questionnaires designed to engage senior managers in this type of discussion must be challenging and sufficiently controversial to inspire interest among even the most cynical management team. Here is an extract from the questionnaire that we used for the senior management of one of the UK's largest commercial banks.

Figure 10.1 Bank Questionnaire

Communication of recent developments to staff

1   Please note the three main developments in the Bank that have most affected the organisation over the last six months

i _____

ii _____

iii _____

2   How were these developments communicated to staff?

_____

_____

_____

3   On a scale of 1 - 5 (5 being well understood) how well do you believe that they understand them?

i   1   2   3   4   5

ii   1   2   3   4   5

iii   1   2   3   4   5

Existing communication practices

1   What communications processes/activities exist in your region/department?

_____

_____

_____

2   How effective do you believe these processes/activities are for communicating strategic and organisational issues?

_____

_____

_____

Figure 10.1 Continued

3   How would you define your responsibility for formal communications in your region/department?

_____

_____

_____

4   Put yourself in the position of a junior member of staff. From their point of view how do you believe you would most like to learn about key developments in the company?

_____

_____

_____

5   What are the issues that you believe contribute either positively or negatively to the communications process in the Company? (culture, attitudes, experience, abiality etc)

_____

_____

Staff attitudes

1   To what extent do you believe that you understand the attitudes of staff within your region/department? Please indicate on a scale of 1 - 5 (5 being total understanding)

          1   2   3   4   5
          └─────┴─────┴─────┴─────┘

2   What do you believe these attitudes are?

_____

_____

_____

3   How do you know? What mechanisms do you have in place to understand/assess staff attitudes?

_____

_____

_____

By exploring how effective current communications are, as well as the implications of new strategies, we successfully managed to focus attention on communications.

ASKING THE RIGHT QUESTIONS

The most valuable audits are those conducted among the entire staff, so that the whole organization takes part in a referendum. But the audit of any balanced sample can test how much key messages have filtered down to staff, whether staff believe them, and whether they think the organization can achieve what they say they can. They can ask staff about existing channels of communication and whether they find them useful.

A questionnaire like this was sent recently to a sample of a motor manufacturer employees. Among other questions, it asked:

Figure 10.2 Motor manufacturer Questionnaire

1 Please tell us how much you agree or disagree with the following statements. *(please tick one box for each statement)*

	Strongly agree	Agree	Disagree	Strongly disagree
• I have confidence in the future of the company.	☐	☐	☐	☐
• We are an innovative company, leading the industry with our products.	☐	☐	☐	☐
• I have a strong interest in how we perform compared to the competition	☐	☐	☐	☐
• We are a company which cares for its employees.	☐	☐	☐	☐
• I often discuss the Company with friends who are not employees.	☐	☐	☐	☐
• What happens to the company is important to me	☐	☐	☐	☐

Figure 10.2 Motor manufacturer Questionnaire continued

2   There are many different ways in which we get information about the Company. How useful do you find the following at present?

(please number the following from 1 to 4 in order of usefulness; 1 = most useful)

• External communications (eg newspapers, TV and radio) ☐

• Briefings by supervisors and managers ☐

• Internal communications (eg newsletters teletext and videos) ☐

• Other sources *(please specify)* ☐

---

3   How good do you think the following types of communications are in the company? *(please give each of the following categories a score; 1 = excellent, 2 = good, 3 = bad , 4 = very bad)*

• Describing the present competitive situation ☐

• Explaining the Company's objectives ☐

• Two-way communication ☐

4   Overall, how satisfied are you with the information you receive about the Company?

• Very satisfied ☐   • Satisfied ☐

• Not very satisfied ☐   • Not at all satisfied ☐

Audits can also ask staff about their relationship with their employers and try to find out what determines it. The European operations of a US industrial gas giant the company used the following questions to give managers a clear picture of the improvements they could make.

Figure 10.3 Gas company Questionnaire

A   My work

Please indicate the extent to which you agree (+) or
disagree (-) with the following statements.

Agree   Disagree
(++) (+) (-) (- -)

• I like the kind of work I do

• My job makes good use of my skills and abilities

• My work gives me a feeling of personal accomplishment

• I am satisfied with the recognition I receive from my
  immediate supervisor/manager for doing a good job

• All things considered, I am satisfied with my job

B   Opportunities for me in the Company

Please indicate the extent to which you agree (+) or
disagree (-) with the following statements.

Agree   Disagree
(++) (+) (-) (- -)

• I am satisfied with the varied opportunities I have to
  do different jobs in the company

• I believe that I will be able to achieve all of my career
  ambitions in the company

• There is a good chance that, within the next year, I will
  leave the company for a better position elsewhere

C   Planning my career

Please indicate the extent to which you agree (+) or
disagree (-) with the following statements.

Agree   Disagree
(++) (+) (-) (- -)

• I understand the way that promotion decisions are made in
  the company

• My immediate supervisor/manager is aware of my
  career ambitions

• This is a good company in the way that it
  plans, monitors and develops the careers of its employees

• I am confident that in the company the right people
  get promoted to the right position at the right time

GETTING THE QUALITATIVE DATA

A questionnaire alone is not enough to assess staff attitudes accurately. Staff should be able to speak directly about how they feel and why, so that researchers can get an accurate picture of relationships inside the organization. This picture must be shown to the management team together with the statistical data from the questionnaire. The biggest problem is that people tend to look more at the statistical data than they do at the qualitative analysis of what people said in face-to-face discussions. This is serious because the qualitative data is the most powerful and, without doubt, if properly collected the more accurate.

Discussion groups are difficult to distort, but when people are being asked to tick boxes against a prescribed set of answers, their understanding of what each box stands for can differ widely – their preferred response to the question may not be an option or they may just sabotage the results by compiling a questionnaire response that does not honestly reflect their views. That is why questionnaire audits should always be supported by group discussions where staff from all parts of the organization participate in confidential discussions with a researcher.

When managements discard the qualitative data in favour of 'hard' statistics, they may use the excuse that the two sets of results do not appear to match. Staff discussions in one company showed tremendous irritation with continual cost-cutting when managers were increasing their demands for more productivity and better quality. Staff were at boiling point and aggression was likely to erupt at any moment. Yet the statistics showed that 95 per cent of staff were satisfied with their work – an exceptional response without any doubt – and it gave the chief executive the excuse to discard the implications of the discussion groups. The discrepancy arose because the statistics were based on staff feelings about their employment histories – which had generally been very positive – while the discussions were directed to the immediate situation.

If the chief executive reported back that all was well because 95 per cent of staff had said they were satisfied with their work, it was likely to be the straw that broke the camel's back.

Of course questionnaires have real value. They are an opportunity to canvass a large number of employees. They provide statistics which can be used in the future to measure change, and to compare the strength of feeling in different parts of the organization.

The qualitative part of the survey needs to be done with care. Individual interviews should be conducted with senior managers. Focus groups, ideally comprising eight to ten people, should last from two to four hours if a real depth of understanding is to be obtained. All levels of the hierarchy and all the different functions should be represented, but it is not necessary to cover every location.

A relatively small number of people need to be consulted during a qualitative process. Whatever the size of the organization, it would be rare to involve more than, say, 100 people or 5 per cent of the workforce for example, in group discussions – because experiences and concerns tend to be similar around the organization.

Qualitative research can also act as a catalyst. Engaging people in debate, capturing their interest, and involving them in the process, are all essential parts of the overall task of which the research should be seen to be part.

If research is going to shift attitudes and change behaviour, the participants must understand what it is trying to achieve in advance. This is as true of managers as it is of staff. You should involve a wide group of managers in agreeing the questions you want, and in piloting the questionnaire among a small number of staff to test for clarity or ambiguity.

It is particularly important to consult the heads of departments if you intend to test employee reaction to any of their initiatives. Otherwise you run the risk, later in the process, of nervous executives complaining that they were not asked to contribute and giving little credence to the results.

GETTING FEEDBACK TO MANAGERS

Senior and middle managers should also be engaged in a consultative process, so that they are provided with the feedback of the research, but also, and more importantly, so that they become part of the improvement process. Relaying the findings becomes the first stage in the process of implementation.

The challenge for the corporate communicator is to build understanding among teams of managers which can then be used as springboards from which to introduce change more broadly across the organization. This can only be achieved with a carefully planned programme of feedback and debate about the research.

Towards a Communication Action Plan

This debate is best done, as we said in Chapter 8, by setting up a series of local management discussions at every key location throughout the organization. The findings of the research should be reviewed, as well as an analysis of the data about that part of the operation. The managers should be asked to work in small groups to find out the cause of the difficulties that the research has uncovered. Then either in small teams again – although with different mixtures of personalities – or as a collective management group, the managers should create what is typically called a Communication Action Plan. This should lay down actions that need to be taken to overcome the problems, allocate responsibilities for these and detail a timetable with in-built reporting deadlines.

FEEDBACK TO SPECIALISTS

The 'not invented here' syndrome is the greatest enemy of good research.

Do not be too prescriptive when you are advising specialists in the organization about the results of the survey and how they affect their particular areas. People responsible for specific initiatives do not like being told how to improve their performance.

Yet improvement is the main aim of the audit. It is best achieved by slow diplomacy that builds a case for change and carries along the specialists on the wave of shared expectation about what can be achieved. So:

- Involve a wide span of senior managers covering all key functional areas.

- Get the managers to commit themselves to feed back results to staff.

- Tell staff that the results will be made available to them and keep to the deadline you have published.

- Give only the results to management in your early discussions with them. Allow them to think through and develop plans for change and development for themselves.

- Do not let managers abdicate their responsibility for deciding what to do next. Recognize that the next step is to gain a broader ownership of the results of the survey and a shared determination of what to do about it.

- Set up 'task forces' empowered to explore the audit's findings across an agreed set of issues and to decide on action.

- Agree with senior management that the feedback should include:
  - A detailed but popularized version of the results, either in a staff newsletter or as a specially created staff news-sheet.
  - A series of meetings for all staff to discuss the results with each relevant management team.

SUMMARY – BUILDING THE CASE

- As people experience improvements, they continue to demand even more.

- You can only get an accurate measurement of success by combining factual and personal measurements. Audits that concentrate on just one dimension will not provide you with the understanding you need.

- The secret of success is to start by getting the whole issue of better internal communication onto the management agenda.

- Engaging people in debate, capturing their interest and involving them in the process, are all essential parts of the overall task of which the research is part.

- Managers should create a Communication Action Plan.

- Improvement is best achieved by slow diplomacy that builds a case for change and carries along the specialists on a wave of shared expectation.

11
Improving Internal Communication: A Practical Guide

You can now put the last four chapters together to improve
internal communication in your company. Six steps towards
improving internal communications.

UNDERSTANDING THE PROBLEM

When an organization complains that its communications are not
working, it is usually describing a symptom rather than the
underlying problem. The solution usually lies not so much in
tinkering with the communication levers, but in a fundamental
change process that the whole organization must go through.

Improving communication demands a reappraisal and probably
a redesign of the organization's basic systems and structures. The
challenge needs to be identified by a broad coalition of senior
managers who also need to investigate fully the implications of
managing the improvements.

A 'Task Definition Session' is a good way of achieving this
shared understanding. This is a full or half day seminar where senior
management are asked to consider the organization's market
positioning and the reputation it needs to get there. They can then

look at the organization's approach, and the impact that this has on staff attitudes and their relationship with their managers – and the changes they believe will be required.

No process of improvement can succeed unless the managers who need to promote it also understand it and feel they have contributed to its development. They are the ones who can best identify the problem and if they are involved, they 'own' changes in the areas where they are responsible.

IDENTIFYING THE COMMERCIAL RATIONALE

Active support for real change must be built on the basis of the commercial advantage that should result.

Organizations which deliberately try to involve employees more and invest in improving their internal communication, find that staff tend to be more innovative, more confident about new ideas and more ready to accept new ways of doing things. Improved communication tends to break down organizational barriers, calm tensions and help staff work with change because they can understand it.

It is also a defence against hostile takeover bids. During an unwelcome bid, staff and management reactions to the approach will be so hostile that even the most resolute of pursuers are likely to rethink their strategy. Observing this reaction, shareholders are likely to be more loyal. They will not want to back a loser. In a friendly merger the value of loyal staff and a unified management will be reflected in the value of a cash deal or share swap.

DESIGNING THE APPROACH

You will need to satisfy the second column of the 'engaging management' diagram opposite by finding a way of debating the objectives and implications with relevant managers.

The management of one of Britain's leading retail banks wanted their communication to become open, clear, two-way, simple, consistent, responsible, timely, regular and honest. They made a

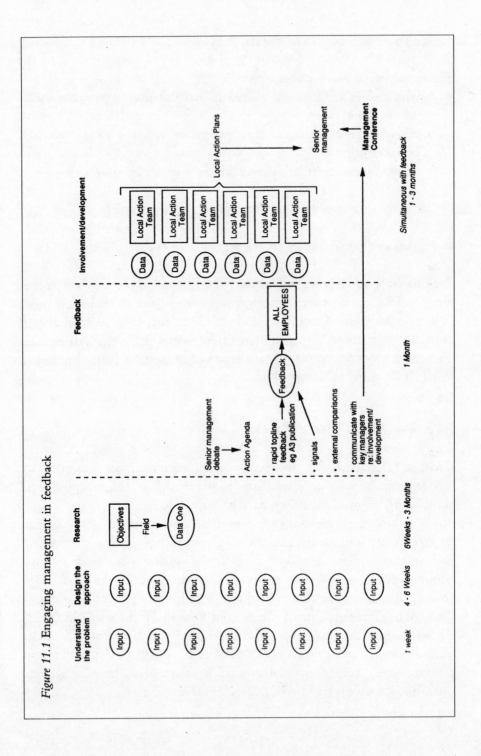

Figure 11.1 Engaging management in feedback

pledge to all 45,000 of their staff. It was:

Top management make a pledge to
- *enable each of us in our daily work to make those changes necessary to keep the Bank ahead*
  - *providing candid information on subjects important to all of us quickly and truthfully*
  - *extending this spirit of openness to the way we all treat each other*

- *show we mean what we say through leading by example*

- *discuss and report openly on the performance of our business*

Laudable as they sound, these words were always going to be meaningless until their implications were fully reviewed and everyone had peered into the Pandora's Box that they were likely to open up. Members of top management were challenged to debate these issues by concentrating on a series of questions, including those shown in Figure 11.2, opposite.

MANAGING THE PROCESS

Change is challenging. It needs the authority of the majority of senior managers to let specialists involve others in developing and promoting an understanding of what is needed.

It is also a process, and it must be co-ordinated with similar programmes which already exist. For example, in a diversified organization there are likely to be a variety of local quality programmes going on at any one time as well as perhaps some overall initiatives such as re-evaluation of human resource strategy. The change process must be managed in association with these.

Managing the change process should be structured to reflect the various levels of involvement required. These are usually top management, central specialists and local implementers, together with people involved in any related reviews.

Figure 11.2 Senior management Questionnaire

Top down communications

Identify the primary sources of key business information in the Bank.

Is there sufficient interaction between them for planning effective delivery of co-ordinated messages? If there is, through what mechanisms? If not, why not? How do you believe more interaction could be encouraged and sustained?

If you were starting from scratch and given the proliferation of primary sources of key business information:

1   How would you define the role of any formal communications group within the Bank?

2   How would you ensure that any formal communications group gets access to the information that it needs?

3   Would you have a central communications team(s)? If yes, why? If not, what would you put in its place and why?

What will enable information to be communicated quickly and truthfully? What may stop this happening at the moment?

Management style

When we talk about 'improving communications' in the Bank, what exactly does this mean? How do you interpret 'communications' in this context?

What type of information must be kept confidential and why?

To whom must it remain confidential?

When can others be advised about it?

Employees in the Bank will be reviewing the 'spirit of openness' and the way we treat each other' later in the year. How would you design an element of the appraisal process that would encourage and support individuals to promote this (new) spirit and evaluate whether or not they have been true to it.

Operational issues

How broad should the invitation be to everyone to define the changes they would like to make?

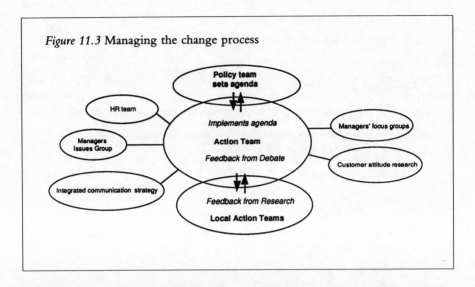

Figure 11.3 Managing the change process

The whole change process should be headed by a *Policy Team* including members of the most senior management forum, ideally chaired by the chief executive. They have to establish the scope of the project, to review it continuously, and to provide an effective two-way channel of communications between the Policy Team and those responsible for implementing the agenda it has set. (Figure 11.3)

Making the agenda come to life should be the responsibility of an *Action Team*. It should comprise a small number of specialists and general managers with particular interests in the activities likely to be affected by the programme. It might for example include the most senior corporate communicator, the personnel director, a divisional general manager and – if there is one – the manager of the total quality programme.

To keep the momentum going, representatives of the Policy Team should report back monthly to the most senior executive management group.

MANAGING THE HUMAN AND ORGANIZATIONAL DIMENSIONS

This probably needs a special *Human Resource Team* which should, under the guidance of the Policy Team, review the organization's existing policies in the light of the improvements and changes that are being sought. This requires a complete understanding of the feelings and aspirations across the organization, and therefore a well-constructed and professionally managed research process within the organization.

It may also need to be linked to an analysis of external views about the organization. This allows you to check internal views about what outsiders think of the organization and the service it provides. It also makes sure that later changes are in the customers' interest.

The research will provide useful intelligence on the prevailing 'culture' of the organization and of the differences that exist between the centre's way of doing things and the ways of the different fields of operation. This in turn should help define the most appropriate style of communications and the degree of control that will need to be exerted from the centre – or alternatively, that control should be avoided at all costs.

The research results must be fed back to the organization. Its conclusions should be used to stimulate a debate about the changes needed and what they will mean for individual responsibilities and organizational relationships.

The results should first be reviewed in full by the organization's top management. They should outline a series of principles for achieving any shift. These principles and objectives should then be communicated broadly to all employees in the organization. These steps are covered under the 'research' and 'feedback' headings of Figure 11.1.

SUSTAINING THE CHANGES

The changes can only last if they are fully understood and fully owned by everyone who is being asked to create them. A simple request from the centre to change work practices is unlikely to generate any change at all, however well meaning the intention.

A two-fold approach is needed to manage the debate and to create the understanding, ownership and momentum that is required to drive change from the bottom up:

- First, you should make an opportunity for local management to hear the detailed analysis of the research into their part of the organization – and help them to think about what it means for their own style of management, and their responsibility to make changes.

- Second, junior members of staff need to make their contribution. One approach that works is setting up *Local Action Teams* to review the changes that are needed – in the light of the research – and to outline two agendas for change: one local, and the other changes in management systems they need to underpin local improvements.

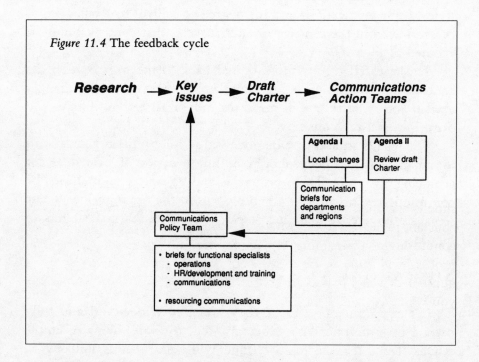

Figure 11.4 The feedback cycle

The Local Action Teams should not work in isolation. They should be and feel part of a larger family of Local Action Teams. They should be structured to overlap. The structure that you choose should reflect your organization's structure, and should encourage two-way flows of information between groups of different teams at different levels of the organization's structure. The diagram illustrates how representatives can link them together across the organization.

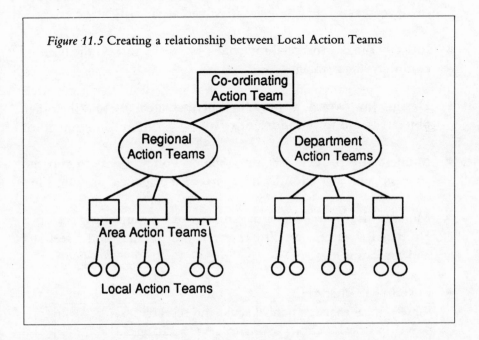

Figure 11.5 Creating a relationship between Local Action Teams

The pressures for change are constantly evolving and these should provide some parameters of the change programme. It needs constant review and re-evaluation in the light of the changing market conditions and on-going developments in business strategy. The process will have to be a key part of the organization's life for a number of years if you are to get the full benefits of the reputation you want.

SUMMARY – IMPROVING INTERNAL COMMUNICATION: A PRACTICAL GUIDE

Six steps to remember:

- **Understand the problem:** set up Task Definition Sessions for management so that they are involved at an early stage.

- **Identify the commercial rationale:** build support on the basis of commercial advantage.

- **Design the overall approach:** Get management to debate the objectives and implications of change.

- **Manage the process:** set up a senior Policy Team to run the process, and an Action Team to make the agenda come to life.

- **Manage the human and organizational dimensions:** set up a Human Resource Team to research the organization's feelings and aspirations.

- **Sustain the changes:**
  – Help local management discuss the research.
  – Set up Local Action Teams to review changes.

Part Four

Managing External Communication

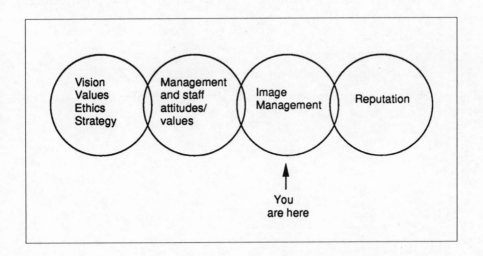

12
The Power of External Communication

Organizations face enormous pressures when they try to be heard in the marketplace. Why we need to develop external communication beyond encouraging people to recognize products, and into the communication of corporate values.

The way organizations manage their external communications is generally much better developed than their efforts to communicate with their own employees.

It is a strange company where the personnel director has greater clout at the boardroom table than the marketing director. And rightly so. Without the sales and a clear understanding in the customer's eye, there is no company.

This has always been the case. As trade developed in early times, groups began to identify with guilds to represent their interests and lend a recognizable corporate clothing to their businesses. Potential customers could then recognize their skills immediately. Even if you could not read or write, you could recognize the pawnbroker by the three brass balls hanging outside his shop, or the barber by the red and white spiral striped pole above the door.

But since Victorian times, corporate venturers have increasingly tried to move away from being seen as 'one of the trade' and have tried to differentiate themselves so that customers will buy their product or service in preference to that of their rivals.

The trend is more pronounced today than it has ever been. Differentiation is vital. The much heralded dawn of uniform global marketing campaigns has proved to be false for all but a few products. We have come to reject commodity items in favour of branded goods. Increased wealth brings a desire to identify with a particular set of values to set ourselves apart from the rest and to make this manifest in the way we live. We expect to choose a product that has been moulded to our lives, rather than the other way round.

We may wince at being labelled 'yuppies' or 'dinkies', or as being sustenance driven or achievement-orientated, but marketeers have benefited from sophisticated tools of analysis that help them to segment markets and pinpoint groups of likely customers. They can now develop advertising campaigns and sales approaches that speak to small groups in their own language – a language that is often being pushed to extremes.

How, for example, are visitors to Britain to know that a photograph of a large expanse of purple silk with just a small neat incision in the middle is advertising a brand of low tar cigarettes?

The Italian knitwear company Benetton takes customer communications to an even higher level of obscurity. Magazines have run advertisements illustrating the 'United Colours of Benetton' with neat rows of condoms in bright primary colours and not a Benetton product in sight. Benetton assumes that its system of customer communication is already so well developed that it only needs to indulge in 'reminder' advertising. The product is expected to be understood by the reader so that the advertisement's only task is to imply that the clothing range is 'of today'.

Product advertising is only the tip of the iceberg. The retail banking market has become enormously competitive in recent years: it has been proven that the average bank customer is much more likely to change marriage partner than to change banks. No wonder all the subtle arts of the corporate marketeer are brought in to play.

In reality the customer knows that this has cost the banks dear. Slim margins cut to attract the notoriously inert personal customer are now forcing banks to cut their branch networks and look again at the way their bank charges are structured.

Customers are unlikely to be fooled for long by humorous or trendy advertising if the day-to-day experience does not match up to the projected image. They are likely to base their decision on the whole experience of dealing with the organization, including such factors as:

- Whether there is a branch nearby.

- The range of services.

- Special deals available at the time.

- Media coverage of the bank's performance or vulnerability to takeover.

- Direct experience of dealing with counter staff.

- The experience of family and friends.

Not to mention the bank's overall reputation. It has taken Barclays some time to recover – at least its image – from the bad press it received from connections in South Africa which were so publicly held against it in the 1970s, and to rebuild its market share among students.

Because of this, external communication has to go way beyond advertising or sales promotion. Our decisions are made in response to a range of stimuli, all of which can be managed as part of a complex system of relationships and interactions.

THE MOST ADMIRED COMPANIES

Let's look first at the nature and size of the task. In January 1991, *The Economist* published a survey of the most admired companies.

Working with Loughborough University, the research team asked 1,800 British businesspeople to name their corporate heroes. Their answers were used to draw up a list of the outside perceptions which seemed to contribute to a positive image:

- Quality of management.

- Financial soundness.

- Quality of products and services.

- Ability to attract, develop and retain top talent.

- Value as a long term investment.

- Capacity to innovate.

- Quality of marketing.

- Community and environmental responsibility.

Top of the list, perhaps unsurprisingly, came Marks & Spencer. One of the most striking things about a company which rates so highly in our national consciousness is that it does not use advertising to get its message across. Its reputation is built on product quality, above all else, but also because we all know it treats its employees exceptionally well, providing many fringe benefits such as chiropody, dentistry and hairdressing to make life easier for its sales staff.

'The culture of our business,' says Marks & Spencer's 1990 annual report, in an unusually frank statement, 'is progressing from paternalism to partnership.' Corporate literature is heavily punctuated with information on the company's non-commercial activities. The pack handed out to new recruits contains a leaflet called 'A Company of Values' which traces the company's history and explains the basis of its management style.

The greatest measure of Marks & Spencer's success has been how easily it has been able to transfer its good name in clothing and food into the more difficult area of financial services. The Marks & Spencer Chargecard is the third largest chargecard operation in the country and the company has also successfully developed unit trusts, a PEP savings scheme and personal loans. Customers trust the brand.

Also ranking high in the *Economist* survey are companies that keep an aura of benevolent paternalism from the past, like Wellcome and Cadbury Schweppes, and those which trumpet their concern for the environment (Tesco and Shell) or support for education, the arts and the community (J. Sainsbury) or that are seen to possess top quality management (S.G. Warburg and Unilever).

'Solid profits and a strong balance sheet help make a great company,' the *Economist* concluded. 'But they may not be enough to make it admired. Admiration counts.'

To compete with the best, organizations are expected not only to be good corporate citizens but to communicate their management ethos and corporate values.

SILENCE IS NO LONGER AN OPTION

There has been an explosion in the various kinds of pressures placed on organizations to communicate better. The bloody dawn raid battlegrounds of the avaricious asset-strippers have taught companies about the importance of clear communication, about corporate strategy, management and performance prospects.

At the year end, the chairman of one major international company – held in private hands until the early 1970s – used to pass the single sheet of final company accounts around the board members attending the meeting for their approval. He was then, as now, a family member. No copies were made for them to look at individually and none were released afterwards. Today of course the City has forced radical changes in practice, but the tremendous sense of secrecy has lived on in the company – with the result that aspiring go-ahead managers are hard to retain and those that are left tend to be obedient rather than innovative. Even now, with the share price failing to match the company's trading performance, the corporate hawks are circling.

Flexible work practices, widely devolved management structures, outworking, the shrinking of corporate functions in favour of buying in consultants or support services – all make it harder to communicate an organization's proposition. In markets where the cost of entry is particularly high or the required investment in technology so great that it is difficult for one organization to assume the sole risk, we are seeing more strategic alliances or network relationships between organizations. Drawing a line around the organizational entity and saying 'this is the company' is increasingly difficult.

CORPORATE TRANSPARENCY

The proliferation of communication media has made it all the harder for communication to be effective.

The huge force of public opinion is not new, affecting political decisions from the poll tax to American pit bull terriers. Even the smallest double glazing firm runs the risk of being pilloried by Esther Rantzen on a consumer rights television programme if it can be shown to have treated the customer badly. This phenomenon, in turn, has given rise to a whole new business vocabulary: 'corporate ethics' and 'social responsibility' are starting to be discussed around boardroom tables.

There is a new magazine in the USA with a circulation of over 7,000 called *National Boycott News*, targeting what the *Wall Street Journal* calls 'ultra conscientious consumers' and alerting them to industrial practices and events which the ethically pure ought to know about, so that they can make informed choices about what they buy. Hence:

- A well-known brand of luncheon meat is out because the manufacturer reputedly indulges in unfair labour practices.

- Investing in a well-known manufacturing conglomerate is out because one of its subsidiaries manufactures nuclear weapon components.

- Drugs produced by a major pharmaceutical group are out because their sale of infant formulas in the Third World is thought to discourage mothers from breastfeeding.

One of the most visible successes of this type of public campaigning is the move to stop McDonalds using styrofoam containers.

The Americans have come up with a new term – the buycott – for active attempts by consumers to buy from conscientious companies and avoid those where the manufacturers' ethics are in doubt. The Body Shop in the UK, for example, champions the idea of non-animal tested products and refillable containers. However, any visit to a Body Shop outlet will make plain that the public's appetite for recycling still has a long way to go: most are in love with the idea more than the practice and few return for refills.

So the ultimate question for corporate communicators is how to reconcile short-term promotions – to shift products and achieve their desired market position – with the longer-term requirement to play a role as a member of the community: corporate profit versus corporate impact.

Or, to take a more cynical view, how can they minimize opposition – social, political or competitive – to what they want to do?

CHANGING PEOPLE'S PERCEPTIONS

Many companies reach for the image consultants – be they public relations agencies, corporate identity specialists or communication management consultancies – when they feel they are being mis-judged by the marketplace, by legislators or by the City. What are they trying to achieve?

Some may have experienced a downturn in sales. Or perhaps they are watching regular tracking studies which look at how well they are regarded, and do not like what they see. Others want to introduce new products or enter new markets or are just looking at new ways of increasing market share. The common plea is: 'What can I do to raise my profile?'

Perhaps their underlying request should be described more accurately as: 'How can my vision, values and strategy be articulated so that I can achieve what I want among everyone who is important to the success of my organization?'

In the next chapter we will look at various groups of individuals who might have a role to play in deciding whether an organization thrives or fails. In the meantime, it is worth pausing to think what we mean by 'articulated'.

It is not enough just to publish what the business is trying to achieve. Many service companies, like high street banks and newly-floated electricity and water boards, have recently spent time and trouble producing customer charters. This is a kind of 'bill of rights' for customers about the corporation's responsibilities and usually includes a promise of reparations if the service does not measure up.

Still more have developed mission statements which spell out what the company stands for and what it is trying to do.

But publication in itself is not enough.

In addition to the value these organizations may have derived from the process of putting their mission or vision statement together and reaching a common agreement on the exact wording, much of the benefit derives from using the output as a touchstone for all forms of external communication.

Companies that have successfully engineered a distinct and positive reputation are those that offer a common experience, however people encounter them.

J. P. Morgan's 'global leader' tag or Mercedes-Benz's 'engineered like no other car' do not provoke wry smiles because the experience of the product, the service and the companies' personnel is impressive.

The close match between image and reality also marks out Virgin as different from other long-distance carriers. The company's 'airline of the year' award promoted heavily in advertising, is borne out by innovative thinking about air travellers' needs:

- top quality in-flight entertainment which makes good use of available technology.

- good price deals for the low budget traveller.

- highly competitive packages to ease the stress of frequent business travel, such as the provision of chauffeur-driven cars to and from the airport.

- award-winning food.

Plus the enthusiastic attitude of cabin crews and ground staff who take the concept of service beyond the rote smile which is the result of the training initiatives developed by so many of their competitors.

SUMMARY – THE POWER OF EXTERNAL COMMUNICATION?

- It is harder than ever to be heard in today's marketplace as communication media proliferate, markets segment and customers become more articulate and more critical.

- Organizational structures and flexible working practices are making it difficult to draw a clear line round a corporate entity and communicate what it stands for.

- To be competitive, communication strategies need to balance short-term promotion of products with longer term investment in communicating their corporate values and ethos.

13
Who Are We Trying to Reach?

External communication is about reaching *all* the groups that are important to an organization's success. That is obvious enough – but who are these groups and how can they be reached?

This chapter helps you find the range of audiences that are likely to be influential – either because their actions directly affect the organization's bottom line or because they can influence those who do.

The most important groups for any organization are likely to be the customers and the shareholders. For publicly quoted companies, 'shareholders' must include the rest of the City with all its complicated interaction of youthful analysts, dealers and brokers, commentators, banks, finance houses and other institutional investors. Private investors, sadly, have little say in the running of corporate businesses.

Then there are all the others who are influential, either because they *shape* the environment in which an organization operates – such as central or local government, trade associations and regulatory authorities – or because they *influence* those who take decisions, like the media, pressure groups and other representative bodies or prominent individuals whose views are listened to.

After the customers and the financial community, keeping in with the regulators is all important, especially if you operate in one of the many sectors coming under increasing public scrutiny. In the public utilities, for example, hand in hand with the greater visibility awarded by the status of a plc, goes accountability and openness to pressure groups and the media. The situation is complicated further for them by the universality of their product – water, gas or electricity. In some cases, the industrial user, the domestic user, the community action group and the shareholder may be combined in the same individual.

The Royal Mail faces a similar problem. The letters business holds a vital position in its status as a legal medium – as in 'proof of postage required' – as well as its vital role in communication. The advent of direct marketing on a massive scale has caused volumes to rise substantially, but has also led to a considerable switch of revenues from postal to fax delivery.

What should it do to counter its poor image, tarnished by a patchy record in industrial relations, bureaucracy and the inevitable accusation of 'fixing the statistics' when the organization tries to quote service quality measures?

As one of the country's largest employers and advertising channels, it has to concern itself with business users, domestic users, consumer groups representing both of these as well as employees, trade unions, advertising and direct mail marketeers, lobbying groups, opinion formers and competitor organizations in activities where it does not have a state monopoly.

Most organizations say they have a clear idea of which groups they should be paying attention to. But it is often revealing to ask a company's senior management team to put these outside groups in order of priority and identify how the perceptions of each are formed. Each time this exercise is carried out, a complex pattern of individuals and groups emerges, connected to the organization by a web of direct and indirect relationships.

The exercise has three main benefits. First it illustrates the important role played by a variety of individuals at all levels of the company, who are all points of influence for the way the organization is perceived. It will show that it is not just the responsibility of the salesmen or the customer relations department to shape the customers' perceptions.

Second, it highlights any gap between the importance of target groups and how much attention is paid to them. This will lead to useful questions about the resources allocated to nurturing relationships with key groups.

Third, it shows that so-called 'audience groups' are not always separate and independent of each other. Not all companies will be faced with the overlaps of the electricity company, but most are likely to find it happening to some extent. At the very least the exercise should teach the organization about the importance of integrated communications planning.

Mapping out what external groups think of you is a parallel process to discovering the perceptions of your own employees, as described in the previous section of this book.

Sales performance figures, pilot promotional programmes, customer tracking reports and market evaluation studies are the lifeblood of those who continually need to understand customer reactions. But if we delve below the figures to find out why customers choose one product or service over another, then it gets more interesting. What is it that creates a more positive reputation?

WHO IS IMPORTANT?

Any organization which wants to put together a sensible strategy to change perceptions must first understand:

- How is it currently perceived.

- What most influences those perceptions.

- What communications activities are most effective and how these vary across the groups.

This understanding is not necessarily complex, but it needs analysis and reflection and is likely to involve some form of structured research.

The Example of a Professional Association

The management team of a professional association reached a point where they needed to re-assess their role. The list of groups they came up with were categorized in order of their importance to the organization. These turned out to be:

- Chief executives and their senior management teams, as major business opinion formers.

- Senior managers of member companies.

- The media, as a means of reaching them – and reaching others as well.

Of secondary importance were:

- Parliamentary and regulatory authorities in the UK and Brussels.

- The education sector.

- Lower level managers.

- Professional bodies.

They then adopted a small number of management topics and themes to champion and claim as areas of specific expertise. These were selected from a plethora of current activities, with close reference to the organization's mission, which had been worked out some time before. By taking a long hard look at the people they needed to influence (business decision-makers) and not just the people it was easiest to reach (lower level managers with more time for training courses) they came to a better understanding of how they should allocate time and resources.

The principle of looking for the most important people to reach, rather than the easiest, is simple. But it is surprising how many opportunities are missed because people tend to stick with the relationships or communication activities with which they feel comfortable.

What You Need to Find Out

The next stage is to decide how you find out what you need to know from them, and what research might be able to tell you. The first question is about methodology and the second about scope.

There are two basic methodologies to choose from – qualitative and quantitative. Both have different merits, as we saw in Chapter 10, so you have to choose a combination of the two which matches your objectives.

The trouble is that researching outside groups is not as easy as pinpointing a representative sample of staff. Access is not guaranteed, and it is difficult to produce statistics which are going to persuade everyone, unless you happen to have a finite customer base or want to look at small select groups – like the MPs of constituencies where the organization has its sites.

It is also more difficult to undertake qualitative research. Sessions among outside groups are often hard to get into the diary of busy customers or so-called opinion-formers. The communication surrounding the research project must be excellent to make sure there are enough people taking part to provide meaningful data.

Companies that take the communication process seriously realize that listening is just as important as clarity of expression. As one British Rail colleague is fond of putting it: 'We have all got one mouth and two ears. Things would be much better if we used them in the same proportion.'

WHAT TO ASK

Take care to define your task and objectives in terms of some of the different reasons for doing research:

- Gathering intelligence.

- Measuring the effectiveness of current relationships and communication activities.

- Getting comparative data – between yourselves and the competition or between different parts of the organization.

- Setting benchmarks, against which you can measure your standing or communications in the future.

- Providing a channel to capture opinions or feedback that are not finding their way back to the main management planning or quality control forums in the normal course of events.

Research, in other words, can do more than just test effectiveness of what you are doing at the moment. It can also:

- Test the strengths and weaknesses of an organization's positioning in relation to competitors or the marketplace.

- Test perceptions of its business strategy and management style.

- Find out in what direction the organization is seen to be going with its products, marketing, sales strategy and corporate structure.

- Find out how important the external pressures are from financial and regulatory communities, or shifts in social values and purchase decisions.

In practice, of course, organizations seldom start with a blank page. The need to categorize audiences and test the state of their thinking usually arises because they need to find an answer to a much more specific question.

The Example of Media Natura

Media Natura is a charity set up to provide advice and form a bridge between the media industry and environmental groups faced with media problems. What could it do to be better known and understood?

With funds in extremely short supply, it could not afford to commission external research. The solution was a session with the main members of Media Natura's management team together with a small number of its non-executive board, who between them represented a spread of media and marketing service organizations.

After a structured questioning process, it was able to compile the long list of groups or people that needed to be taken into account when a new communication strategy was developed. More questions revealed that survival depended on only two groups: the media owners – those with influence in newspaper or publishing groups, TV and radio stations or poster site owners – and the campaigning organizations in need of Media Natura's assistance. Proper planning could then be done to devise messages that appealed to these two specific groups. The charity could harness and direct its meagre resources to maximum effect with a small number of highly-targeted activities.

SUMMARY – WHO ARE WE TRYING TO REACH?

- The key to any programme's success is how coherent the picture is which it projects to outside audiences.

- The first step to achieving this coherence is to categorize those you want to influence and what you want them to feel and know about you.

- The second is to launch a process by which the needs of the groups are listened to, understood and then taken into account.

14
The International Dimension

The problems of matching media and message to audience are
the same, from global branding to microniche marketing.
Cultural differences are, however, very real and need to be
properly considered in any integrated communications strategy
that crosses national boundaries.

Recent events in eastern Europe have pushed the issues of sovereignty and cultural definition back into the spotlight.

If the differences between people across boundaries are real, then
what are the implications for organizations who want to build
reputations and sell products or services outside their own national
boundaries or home markets?

Just as a whole new generation has been forced to realize that
'Russia' is not the same as the USSR, so we have also had to rethink some of our own definitions of Britishness. Most large
employers and nationalized industries used to have a 'buy British'
policy for company cars. Many of these have now been relaxed
because a car with a Japanese name is likely to be more 'British' than
some of our traditionally indigenous brands.

Satellite and telecommunication advances have made it easy to keep in touch with the farthest flung parts of a corporate empire, or to react immediately to changing market conditions on the other side of the globe. But there are complications too. Many companies are having to cope with manufacturing in widely separated places for the first time, and to communicate quality and ethical specifications across widely differing cultural groups.

The explosion in media has also made it harder to compete for the market's attention. Communicating your organization's points of difference has never been so important now that consumers have, literally, a world of choice.

EUROSPEAK

In many ways the European markeplace has already arrived, in advance of much of the formal single market legislation. Out goes the macaroni cheese and in comes the tagliatelle burro e salvio. Out goes Maxwell House and in comes frothy cappucino – now conveniently packaged in sachets, just add water. The Dordogne is rapidly turning into a Surrey look-alike. How do we know? Because everyone is driving Swedish-made Volvos.

To some extent the Euro-consumer market has always existed at the luxury end of the market. They were the people who had the money to travel and they imported some of the eating and drinking habits of our continental cousins. But today it is no longer the preserve of the rich and bored. The identikit European business traveller – whether he is a Dubliner or Dutchman – is likely to be wearing an Italian-style off-the-peg suit and a Burberry raincoat, and will be clutching his copies of the *Financial Times* and *The Wall Street Journal*. He has just been to one of the big West End shows in London; last week he went to the Musée d'Orsay in Paris and has recently returned from a ski-ing holiday in Val d'Isère. He probably works for one of the big UK multinationals or a global consulting firm.

Of course he represents only a relatively small proportion of the overall population. 'Abroad' for many still means ten days learning how to windsurf in Lanzarote.

For every international product success story there are more that fail to find favour outside their own national boundaries. On the other hand there are some striking recent examples of products that, without changing their basic offer, have successfully translated into other cultures. The Swedish furniture chain Ikea – a latterday Habitat, which also found success outside the UK market – has identified a gap in the market. Then there is the publishing success story of *¡Hola!* magazine. It started as a modest family venture in Barcelona and rapidly grew into a popular Spanish institution, with a variety of picture stories about the rich and famous. The UK launch has been equally successful. The title has remained the same – *Hello* – and so has the format and policy that interviewees are always treated favourably, without sex or scandal.

Another interesting phenomenon is that the attributes of other countries are often used to market locally-made products, especially food.

Organizations with any kind of international dimension need to think not only about communicating with their current local marketplaces, but also of gathering local intelligence that will assist them in the longer term.

- Are they interested in developing a consistent reputation, as opposed to a local version in each of their countries of operation?

- Are there aspects of their operations that are acceptable in the host country, but would harm their reputation elsewhere if they were publicized?

- What should be the balance between, say, the international corporate 'brand' and local product brands?

- What would be the cost benefit of amalgamating existing local brands into an international one – as when the British Marathon chocolate bars became American-style Snickers?

They also need to think about the implications for the way communications are structured across the business:

- If local offices deal with local media, then who deals with international media on international issues? And on local issues?

- Does it make sense to have a network of different areas of communication expertise, spread across your operations but still working together?

- Should local communication budgets be dictated by local management, and local business performance? Or should there be a mandatory minimum budget and programme at local level, perhaps funded centrally?

- How should the annual programme planning process be structured internationally?

- Have they made enough provision for sharing best practice between sites and countries?

NEW INSTITUTIONS

New communication techniques have broken down barriers and shrunk the world. Even the Albanians recently started to receive Greek television and saw beyond the impenetrable mountain range that had helped the country's repressive regime isolate its population.

Information has never been so widely available. Phone, fax and modem-linked computers mean that physical location is becoming less important. But sometimes it is not a question of making use of these new media, but of organizing resources in such a way that their penetrating reach can be countered.

If customers in Arkansas can hear about a plant accident in the Indian sub-continent within 12 hours, or if a pressure group uses world-wide media to attack a company's Third World ethics, then the organization's management team must be in a position either to beat the news – probably out of the question for all but the most sophisticated of multi-nationals – or to have a full and satisfactory response in hand. Otherwise there will be a loss of confidence or sales.

Apart from the media, national and international companies have a number of new regulatory or political organizations to take into account. The most obvious of these is the European Commission and all that implies, including the European Parliament and other Brussels institutions.

Most large organizations have been planning for some time for this new regulatory environment. Some, like BP and Levi Strauss, have moved the centre of their European operations to Brussels. Others, like Philip Morris, keen to keep close to what is now the focal point for the anti-tobacco lobby, have sent their public affairs function there. Pressure groups have also moved quickly to capitalize on this growing internationalism and these new political seats of power.

THE IMPLICATIONS FOR COMMUNICATIONS

First, organizations need to make sure their communication functions are, at the very least, aware of the international repercussions of local activities. They must also know what to do to reach all their important groups, wherever they may be.

They need to understand local sensitivities. There is a famous story about the Bank of America's US advertising agency, which dreamt up a global advertising campaign with the catchline 'Follow the leader'. Their local German team in Frankfurt spotted this only just in time to change the copy before it went into the local media as 'Verfolgen Fuhrer'.

To prevent such embarrassments and maximize local abilities, there needs to be shared agreement about the division of responsibilities between local, national and international communication functions. This has to be understood internally and communicated to all those who need to know outside the organization.

Finally, there must be rapid lines of communication between different countries to make sure news can be spread quickly, and the implications for each part of the organization assessed and communicated to relevant local management teams.

SUMMARY – THE INTERNATIONAL DIMENSION

- Communications technology means that organizations can communicate the same message at the same time to all their target audiences. At the same time, small groups are increasingly concerned with identifying their own unique culture.

- Organizations need to decide how best to communicate basic values and ideas across these widely different cultural groups, and how much consistent reputation is necessary or possible.

- Organizations must find a balance between the corporate 'brand' and the local products or company brands in each marketplace.

- They also need to translate this into central and local communication responsibilities and allocate appropriate resources for each.

15
Developing Strategy

Managing external communication is like managing anything
else. Yet companies may have relied for too long on intuition
for their communication activities, or let themselves be guided
by external advisers more than they would allow in other areas.
They seldom set clear objectives or measure results. Should
communication be left to the experts? And how do you develop
a strategy and programme?

The fact that we can list some of the influences on a company's
reputation suggests that it is possible to have some control over it,
and that we can change people's views and behaviour towards us by
planning our communications better.

A communication strategy is the way that an organization:

- Formulates and articulates a clear vision of what it is there to do.

- Knows the groups of people it needs to reach and influence.

- Listens to those groups to find out how it is thought of and how
  this can be improved.

- Shapes a programme to reinforce, enhance or change these
  views.

CREATING GENUINE DIFFERENCE

The first goal of any strategy should be to create a genuine sense of differentiation among outsiders. There are few prizes for being ranked alongside everyone else, with no distinguishing features worthy of comment. Life is usually too short to be subtle. (Clarity and precision are the surest way to rapid understanding.)

Organizations today have to compete for attention through a barrage of 'noise', so making an impression means honing down what you are saying to an absolute minimum. This often means reducing a complicated sales message to a single line or phrase, like the classic Saatchi campaign slogan which helped the Conservatives win power in 1979: 'Labour isn't working'. Or the series of arresting full page press advertisements: 'I think therefore IBM'.

Everything that an organization says about itself, every activity it engages in, are all part of what it communicates. The purpose of a strategy is to compress and reinforce the main ideas that it wants to get across to the groups most influential for its success.

THE TOOLS OF THE TRADE

Communications activities at any organization's disposal, over and above straightforward marketing and sales, include:

- Relationships, from the treatment of guests and visitors to the maintenance of long-term suppliers and partners.

- Recruitment.

- Advertising.

- Specific marketing support techniques, like sales promotion, exhibitions or hospitality events.

- Corporate identity.

- Public relations – including product, brand, company, corporate and financial.

- Community relations.

- Sponsorship and charitable activities.

- Parliamentary and government affairs – national, local, European and international.

In most organizations, the responsibility for these activities may be split between marketing, public relations or public affairs, personnel or human resources, as well as the secretariat or chief executive's office.

There is a world of difference between marketing support as defined by McDonalds – with special offers for kids or initiatives to keep the pavements outside their shops free of litter – and by Citibank which designs seminars and publishes market analyses to help the bank's 'relationship managers' cement their trading relationships.

Community relations for many large property developers has meant putting resources into local schools and construction skills training centres for the local unemployed. Their message is clear: 'Our development is going to disrupt your community, but we will do our best to make sure it also provides you with new opportunities'.

Marketing programmes have attracted big budgets and therefore serious attention at the most senior level. It is all the more worrying, therefore, that some of these budgets are actually mis-spent. At best, they are not as integrated as they could be, but are divided among concepts like corporate identity, advertising and PR.

CORPORATE IDENTITY

This has been an increasingly popular answer to the problem of market definition in the past decade, although some would argue that the design community has benefited more than their corporate clients. It has however, helped organizations to look critically at the verbal and visual language they use and how parts of their organization are seen to relate to each other.

It is important that companies think about corporate identity in its widest sense before they decide what changes, and therefore what outside help from agencies, are most appropriate for them. The corporate identity specialists operating near the management consultancy end of the spectrum would define identity as:

- The organization's name, the *structure* of names representing its parts, subsidiaries and brands, and how these inter-relate.

- The visual *style* as expressed through its products, printed materials including packaging and stationery, its working environments and the livery of its staff, vehicles etc.

They might also include the *behaviour* of employees and the style of language employed, but none of the design-led companies have made many inroads here so far. Apart from specific design management skills, training and development work still tend to be the preserve of human resource departments.

Communicating the intangible 'company' that lies behind the product becomes all-important as advances in communication and technology have caused products to converge rather than diversify. This has been fuelled by the massive spate of mergers, buyouts, demergers and takeovers in the past 10 to 15 years, and by privatization which has left many enterprises which used to be publicly owned reaching for the tools of the corporate sector to satisfy more demanding shareholders and customers.

Where the corporate identity boom has been less successful is in the provision of training skills in design management *inside* companies. If the corporate identity is successful, it should not need to be carried out again for many years. The specialist skills, therefore, tend to stay in the agency sector. Once the formal launch and implementation is over, agencies and clients usually part company and a degree of local anarchy within different parts of the company is often inevitable.

The fact that the identity boom coincided with an economic boom has been even more detrimental to the idea. A corporate identity review is often seen as something you do as a one-off in the good times. The widespread criticism of British Telecom's new leaping Pan piper logo, and ICI and BP's multi-million pound tweaks to their letterforms, have done little to further the case of design in shaping perceptions of organizations.

ADVERTISING

More than almost any other sector of the marketing services industry, advertising has suffered from the recent economic downturn. Probably the downturn coincided with what would anyway have been testing time for the traditional advertising industry.

The explosion of new media has cut the cost of media space and tailored products are increasingly targeted at small groups of customers. 'Narrowcast' media like personalized direct mail and affinity group marketing – where customers are identified by their shared interests, such as membership of the National Trust or drivers of certain makes of car – were bound to increase as society tries to return to an increased sense of individual expression.

The advertising industry has indulged in a great deal of discussion about whether there really is such a thing as corporate advertising and agonized over how it can be measured. Sticking the Allied Lyons logo on the end of a series of unrelated product commercials probably did nothing to boost sales, but it would have acted as a gentle reminder to the handful of key institutional advisers who were involved in Allied Lyons' latest bid.

The advertising medium is being used for new purposes. The agencies coming to the fore are those prepared to take a hard-headed and fresh approach to all communication that is occupying their clients and are prepared to work as part of broader multi-disciplinary teams.

PUBLIC RELATIONS

The PR sector suffers along with insurance agents and timeshare salesmen from lack of public credibility. Conscious of this image, the industry has made great strides to professionalize and improve the quality of its recruitment. This has been helped partly by floating the larger businesses and, as a result, addressing the need to tighten up their financial performance and management structures.

The term 'public relations' itself covers a multitude of sins, ranging from basic press relations – which is where the industry began – to highly sophisticated international lobbying campaigns and everything in between.

The industry has recently polarized into a small number of large international companies – often part of larger marketing services groups – and a multitude of 'one man and a dog' operations, content to work for only a handful of clients at any one time. In between these generalists a range of specialists have sprung up offering a range of specific skills and contacts.

Many PR agencies are beginning to cut back their annual retainer fees for keeping a client on their books. In too many cases these had led to a lazy attitude and a drop in standards. By carrying out work which is divorced from a clear set of communications objectives, the industry has laid itself open to criticism for charging fees for no definable results.

PR firms have been slow to accept that communication can be measured like any other management discipline. Recent initiatives to build a computer analysis model to assess the quantity and quality of press coverage is starting to find favour. But if the industry stops short at this, it will be falling into the trap it just started to climb out of. It would view success in terms of volume rather than the client's own organizational objectives.

It is still hard to find examples of agencies that are genuinely taking a strategic overview. This is partly because they need to earn 'mark-ups' on specific activities they carry out on their clients' behalf as opposed to adopting an objective stance. The key questions to ask when you are hiring public relations skills are:

- What will my organization learn from this relationship, and how much will skills be transferred across from the agency?

- Or am I simply looking for extra 'arms and legs' organizational skills on a specific range of tasks?

- What is the real nature of the specialist knowledge I am tapping into?

- How can we best use our combined skills and resources?

There are huge risks in handing the company's communication's activities – or part of them – over to a third party. Having a PR outsider as company spokesman is a dubious idea, certainly in the eyes of the media who tend to take a cynical view of intermediaries.

KEEPING CONTROL

Each one of these three mainstream suppliers of communications – identity, advertising and PR – tend to compete with the others to be the key discipline. All have vested interests in the delivery of some forms of communications over others.

The question of which resources to keep in-house and which to subcontract and the optimal ways of integrating the various disciplines are covered in Chapter 17. There is a range of skills and techniques to be learnt or bought, but sub-contracting control of communication should ideally only be done when you have clarified your objectives and overall communication strategy.

You abdicate this at your peril.

SUMMARY – DEVELOPING STRATEGY

- Developing a coherent external communication strategy needs a clear vision of what the organization is there to do and who it needs to reach and influence.

- Listening to these groups is as important as communicating 'at' them.

- How the various communication techniques work together depends on how clear an organization's communication objectives are, and how these are communicated to agencies that are being sub-contracted to help.

16
The Reality
Behind the Smile

How organizations can strengthen relationships with customers by exceeding their expectations and being known for it.

Customer care has arrived with all the kudos of a new wonder cure and has led to the birth of a whole new industry of suppliers – from advisers on interpreting body language to interactive training techniques for handling customer complaints. Even the government has jumped on the bandwagon with the publication of a series of customer charters, designed to keep key services up to the mark.

Personal and business customers are increasingly looking to their suppliers for quality, accurate forecasts about delivery, and courteous and helpful service. But they are also now looking for a commitment to them – the customer – so that they understand their total requirements and are developing a service to match.

This means getting the straightforward procedural things right such as:

- The tone of voice used on the phone.

- The behaviour of all staff that the customer encounters.

- Response times.

- Compensation for delays and faults.

- Accurate routing of queries.

- Availability of the appropriate staff when the customer needs them.

Organizations can start to improve their performance in all of these areas by developing training in procedures for 'front line' staff, and by increasing the confidence of staff to handle the various situations they are likely to meet.

But there is a bigger question which affects all staff and the organization's reputation among all external groups: 'How is the handling of customers built into the organization's overall offer?'

The Example of Royal Mail Letters

As a first step to understanding its 500,000 business customers better, Royal Mail Letters changed the role of its 200-strong sales force. This team had based its activities on cold calling. This was changed into something more like an account handling structure, where individuals and teams were responsible for specific groups of customers. 80,000 replies were received to their massive postal research programme. As many as 30,000 people wrote comments beyond the specific information they were asked for, about the type of service they would like to receive. This has provided Royal Mail Letters with the first hand information it needed to build a more accurate customer database and to start introducing changes that take customer needs into account. Customer mailings are now a regular part of the marketing programme.

The Royal Mail's changes may be second nature to many. But what is important is that it now sees its business operations as a partnership with customers, and has started to extend the relationship beyond simply delivering the mail properly.

The example of British Airways

British Airways is probably the best-known example of taking charge of customer perceptions in this way – changing its production mentality to putting the customer first. The role that its customer service measures now plays in product development is not so well-documented.

The two functions were merged in 1990 under British Airways' director of marketing and operations Liam Strong. 'We know that if we lose a customer it costs five times as much to get them back as it does simply to maintain,' he told the *Financial Times*.

A continuous customer research programme is undertaken by a 100-person team who conduct 250,000 interviews in 60 airports around the world every year. In-flight surveys collect the responses of a further 80,000 passengers. Additional research is done on an ad hoc basis for specific marketing projects and the company also has a business flyers' panel. The results are used in the development of new brand concepts and service developments.

There is a basic minimum guideline of training at least every 18 months for all employees who have anything to do with service delivery. After this, service is measured for each product in terms of:

- Revenue.

- Yield.

- Number of seats occupied.

- Market share.

- Punctuality.

- Mis-handled baggage.

- Passengers rated as 'very satisfied'.

- Complaint rate per 1,000 passengers.

- Cargo shipped booked.

- Involuntary off-load rate – when customers are allocated to another flight because of over-booking.

- Cleaning standards.

- Catering.

These measures are circulated to senior managers and reviewed monthly. British Airways believes this careful measurement has led to more differentiation between its own products, so that they suit different kinds of air traveller, and better, more accurate product development than rival airlines. The stated reason is that British Airways needs to keep one jump ahead of an increasingly critical customer and to be able to surprise them by anticipating their needs rather than waiting for their complaints.

UNDERSTANDING WHAT IT IS LIKE ON THE RECEIVING END

British Airway's customer service training programmes also offered staff experience of what it was like to work in related job areas next to their own.

'It is remarkable how few companies that have introduced customer care programmes have taken the issue of organizational structure seriously. Yet inappropriate structure is one of the largest contributors to poor service,' said ITEM group chairman David Clutterbuck in *Marketing* magazine (18 May 1989). 'Rigid barriers between functional departments are a major issue. They inhibit cross-discipline task forces, even when someone from above insists they are formed. They focus thinking on parts of problems and prevent the free movements of ideas.'

When Bank of America experienced financial problems in the late 1980s, and new retail customers were hard to attract, head office told all managers to spend time in branches on the phone to customers.

The move was inspired. Keeping existing customers was firmly understood by all to be a number one priority. Staff took heart from the involvement of managers from all levels in the bread-and-butter business of the bank. And managers benefited from opening up their own lines of communication to customers and their own front line staff. The bank now appears to have turned a corner and, although the hands-on experience was only one facet in its turn-around programme, it seems to have achieved it with much of its Californian customer home base intact.

Rowntree Mackintosh in the UK operates a voluntary policy of letting office-based managers spend time on the shop floor. No special provision is made and managers are not allowed to slope off back to management meetings or expense account lunches at meal breaks. They work full shift hours for a week or a fortnight at a time and have to face the same quality control tests and performance measures as their full-time colleagues.

Gateway is one of a number of retail companies to have customer panels to put managers in touch with shoppers. Over 60 customer panels are held every year to allow a cross-section of Gateway customers to discuss store developments with a Gateway management team, normally including one main board director.

SUMMARY – THE REALITY BEHIND THE SMILE

- Customer service depends on getting all the straightforward procedural things right.

- Organizations need to question how much customer care is truly built into the way they operate, in order to be competitive.

- Organizations need not only to track progress but to feed management decision-making about product, marketing, delivery and service strategies.

17
Organizing
For Communications

**If you want to change the way people see your company's goals
and expertise – no matter what size it is – the basic planning
and implementation process will be the same. But how do you
define the communication function, what are its responsibilities,
and how should it be resourced?**

The role of the corporate communicator has started to change
wherever there has been a decision to take control of the reputation,
internally and externally. Until fairly recently those involved were
known as the Public Relations Managers. They held responsibility
for press relations, the company newspaper and were probably also
the chief executive's 'gofer'.

But now, both the title and the seniority of the post are more
likely to reflect a new and wider role, including championing the
importance of communication throughout the organization.

The new heads of corporate communications extend beyond
their traditional turf and take responsibility for feeding ideas into the
corporate planning process. Their two main roles are:

- To be scouts, scanning horizons for issues that are going to affect
  the company's operations.

- To be facilitators, responsible for encouraging various functions across the organization to form coalitions to plan together. Their objective is to get managers to confront the communication implications of their plans and actions and to share information, so that staff reinforce what the organization is trying to achieve.

In a recent survey of 81 senior 'heads of corporate communications' (*The Rise to Power of the Corporate Communicator:* Smythe Dorward Lambert, 1991) a third of them had held their job for two years or less. They tended to comment on a 'new role created because of the sheer size and span of communications' or 'a position created in recognition of the strategic importance of public affairs'.

They are increasingly taking their brief direct from the top: over a quarter reported direct to the organization's chairman and nearly half to the chief executive or managing director.

The communicators stand at a difficult crossroads. They are both insiders looking out and outsiders looking in. As insiders, corporate communicators are uniquely well-informed about the organization's activities, stances and future plans. They understand how the coalitions of power operate and what processes drive strategy. As outsiders, communicators have to be objective about the organization's reputation and how this differs from what it should be. They need to represent the company's interests to influential opinion-formers, including key journalists, where judgements have to be made about handling sensitive information.

They also have to balance acting as a central resource with being an internal adviser or facilitator. As a central resource the communication function can be responsible for a variety of practical activities, from graphic design to industrial relations.

But they are increasingly aware that they need to spend more time at a more strategic level. If communication and employee involvement strategies are to work, then they must reflect the organization's overall business strategy. This means corporate communicators must understand the strategy enough to persuade senior managers of their point of view.

Corporate communicators' role as intelligence scouts means that they must adopt a listening stance. The environment is one area where some companies have had to move fast to reassure customers and regulators. Again, it is ideas-led companies like the Body Shop which have shown the way. Employees were offered company bicycles instead of cars long before the government started to erode the financial benefits of running a company car. Some organizations have clearly been slower off the mark.

MATCHING ORGANIZATIONAL STRUCTURES

What about those who work far from the centre or whose organization has a highly devolved management structure? How does the shape of an organization affect the way communications are managed?

There is a marked trend towards devolved management structures, because they are thought to improve decision-making, speed up responses and motivate local managers. But there are bound to be some grey areas about how much conformity or freedom is allowed in representing the company and creating a distinctive culture locally.

What about those communication specialists in remote places, far from the head office, or deep in diversified areas with little in common with other parts of the group? They may have little to do with investor or parliamentary relations, but they will probably have more impact than the central communicators on a range of activities including marketing support, 'front line' industrial relations and local charity or community initiatives.

All organizations need to ask themselves:

- How much is communication policy set at head office? How much is decided locally? How much is agreed collectively?

- How should head office, the group or the holding company – the centre, wherever it is – be represented in local communications?

- What minimal standards in communication should apply right across the organization? And what encouragement should there be to make sure they are kept to?

For the overall communication strategy to be effective, local communicators have a fundamental role helping to set organization-wide objectives and taking part in the group planning process.

MAIN AREAS TO BE DEVELOPED

There are four main areas to be developed in the short term before any corporate communicator can progress much further:

- Defining and clarifying the communication task better.

- Measuring effectiveness accurately and usefully.

- Winning commitment from all senior managers.

- Developing practical and creative action plans that will genuinely make a difference to strategy and direction.

RESOURCING COMMUNICATIONS

The age when all communication requirements are put into one large centralized department is largely over. Heads of corporate communications typically have fewer people reporting directly to them than would have been the case five years ago. This is not just because of the general shift towards devolving responsibilities and rejecting bureaucracy. It is also because communication is increasingly tested for quality and for cost-effectiveness.

What you need depends on your industry, the stage of corporate growth or on specific public issues. The oil and gas sector, for example, has a long tradition of well-resourced crisis communication teams. They are able to man press offices, co-ordinate rescue facilities and relay information to workers' families and the local community if there is an offshore accident. This means a financial commitment, not just to the size of the team, but also to up-to-date communication links and training for those involved.

Others, like nuclear power operators, need a comprehensive network of local liaison people to consult with local communities and pressure groups.

Communication functions which best support their organization's strategic goals seem to be those with some operational freedom, and which are sensitive to the key issues likely to affect their organization. They are also likely to have in-house specialist skills – or to be able to manage outside suppliers of them. These include:

- Support for the board – including speechwriting, VIP visits and the formulation of management communiqués.

- City and investor relations.

- Government and public affairs.

- Crisis handling.

- Internal communications.

- Public relations.

- Community relations and charitable giving.

- Marketing services or product promotional support.

- Advertising.

- Design management, including corporate identity.

In practical terms, these activities are unlikely to be the sole responsibility of one team and could be spread across a range of functions. A middle-sized industrial manufacturing plc might decide to make these appointments:

- Head of Corporate Communications.

- Investor Relations Manager.

- Press Officer.

- Communication Services Manager.

It would also have communication managers in each of its main operating parts.

Head of Corporate Communications

This function should be concerned primarily with formulating the company's communication policy, and making sure it is implemented effectively throughout the organization. By providing the highest level of communication advice to the board and members of the senior management team, he or she can also support those who are acting as spokespeople for the company.

As part of the public affairs role, a working knowledge of government and parliamentary procedures is important, together with monitoring information sources and the structure of pressure groups and lobbyists in the relevant sector.

Corporate communication heads will thrive if they have easy access to all members of the senior management team, including operational managers in far flung parts of the organization.

Investor Relations Manager

This needs specialist working knowledge of the City and an understanding of reporting requirements of all the stock exchanges where the organization is quoted. The manager also needs to understand disclosure rules and other procedures. Most publicly quoted organizations run briefing programmes for financial analysts, institutional investors and specialist media commentators.

He or she will also need to supervise the publication of interim and annual results and cover all meetings of shareholders, including the AGM.

The main responsibility is to keep in touch with the right fund managers and analysts and make sure the organization keeps its profile in the investment community – that its strategy is understood well and that key senior personnel are known among the major institutional investors.

Press Officer

Good press officers are rare. Their intrinsic difficulty is that they have to act both as promoter and defender of the organization's interests. True to the British penchant for clubs and closed cartels, much of the most effective press work in the UK is done 'behind the scenes', briefing key correspondents off the record and maintaining close relationships with the media. Real news is rarely published in a press release.

But thanks to an equally strong, though patchy, tradition of investigative journalism, companies have good reason to fear a misinformed journalist or a newspaper with a mission to expose and sensationalize. So it pays to have a highly intelligent press officer. This is not, as many companies seem to treat it, a junior job or one that should be wholly delegated to an outsider.

Communication Services Manager

Most organizations feel they need to keep at least some in-house expertise, to oversee the production of corporate brochures, company newspapers, exhibitions, slides and videos.

This list will increasingly be extended to electronic media like e-mail and online 'news' transmission systems, which are likely to be increasingly important in the way companies are structured – and how the parts communicate with each other and with the world outside. Computer networking and telecommunications have already changed the pace of communication in most large organizations and are going to cause the greatest changes in management thinking.

The speed of communication is making editorial control increasingly hard. This makes it all the more important that the 'production' departments – as well as local communication managers –

understand the strategic context of the information they are transmitting.

IN-HOUSE OR AGENCY?

There is little point in going to the expense of adding to the in-house payroll if the necessary skills are only going to be needed for three months out of every twelve.

All suppliers are, ultimately, led by their own bottom line rather than those of their clients. So it is vital that you choose outside advisers according to your objectives rather than the capabilities of the agency. Nobody should be surprised that advertising agencies, for example, are hard-pressed not to include advertising when they are quizzed about a communication strategy.

The most significant trend in the marketing services sector, after the rise and relative fall of the Saatchi and WPP groups' attempts to build one-stop shopping, has been the increasing importance of specialist niches. The idea that global companies or brands would find agencies on a global scale, with strategic planning, research, advertising, marketing, PR, design, sales and so on, all in one integrated group – if not a fully linked network – failed to take into account the national or local brand managers. They tend to prefer being close to their creative centres and not to accept orders on a plate from a remote head office in Minneapolis, New York or London.

Although the few really global brands will continue to seek advice on a worldwide scale from one source, others have to look for a broad range of advice from a broad range of suppliers. Many of these companies are learning fast how to sort the wheat from the chaff, how to find the best specialists and how to co-ordinate their efforts. They are especially keen to operate in a way that supports their communications, rather than encouraging a bloody internecine agency war, fought at the client's expense.

Objectives have to be agreed by both sides at the beginning of the relationship. You must stay watchful to make sure the work is on target, on budget and on brief.

SUMMARY – ORGANIZING FOR COMMUNICATIONS

- The role of corporate communicators needs to change for these processes to work effectively. They need to act as outsiders looking in as well as insiders looking out.

- Their main function is to act as scouts, scanning horizons for issues that may affect the organization's operations.

- They should also be responsible for providing leadership in communication, for encouraging joint planning on communication initiatives across the business and for encouraging managers to confront the communication implications of their plans and actions.

- There are four main areas to be developed in the short term before any corporate communicator can progress much further:
  – Defining and clarifying the communication task.
  – Measuring effectiveness accurately and usefully.
  – Winning commitment from all senior managers.
  – Developing practical and creative action plans that will genuinely make a difference to strategy and direction.

- Communication functions which best support their organization's strategic goals seem to be those with some operational freedom.

- For the overall communication strategy to be effective, local communicators have to help set organization-wide objectives and take part in the group planning process.

- It is vital that you choose outside advisers according to your objectives rather than the capabilities of the agency.

Part Five

Delivering
Practical Programmes

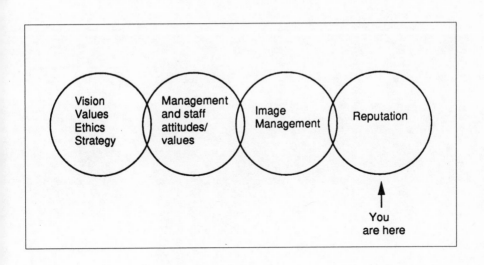

18
Refreshing the Planning Process

How to plan a communication strategy which is integrated into a broader business plan. And how the planning cycle itself can be used to refresh strategy and spread communication programmes widely throughout the organization.

It is sensible – as it is in all management disciplines – to decide what quality standards should be applied across all your communication efforts. You also need to set up measurement techniques to check these standards are being achieved.

The challenge is how to make management responsible for monitoring communication – even those who have no formal responsibility for 'external communications'. But how can standards be built into job assessments, appraisals or review processes on both a corporate and personal level?

How can you measure the role of communication in its effect on relationships with customers, regulators and other external audiences? What, anyway, constitutes a 'satisfied customer'?

MEASURING CUSTOMER SATISFACTION

The key to this is the same as creating the communication strategy in the first place. It means understanding what each target group feels is important about the organization and their relationship with it, how these perceptions are formed and how the relationship or communications can fulfil their potential.

Setting communication budgets and then justifying them usually means using some kind of measurement to test the effectiveness of the activities. Do staff read the company newspaper, for example? Do briefing documents reach the right decision-makers?

As the communication management process roots itself deep in management thinking, corporate communicators realize they must go beyond simple polling techniques. It is the *quality* of relationships which dictate attitudes to an organization, and lead people to buy from it, listen sympathetically to it or work for it effectively.

So measuring is likely to mean asking some of the following questions:

- What are people's attitudes on specific issues?

- What are the effects of current communication systems?

- What sources of information are valued and believed?

- How much does current communication practice match the needs of people at the receiving end – on both a 'need to know' and 'nice to know' basis?

A MODEL PLANNING PROCESS

Here is a step-by-step guide to planning a communications programme, at the same time as measuring it and testing its cost-effectiveness:

- Develop a clear set of communication objectives, closely tied to your organization's business objectives.

- Translate these into a set of annual goals which are specific enough to measure progress, and hold people accountable to them.

- Set priorities in order of the importance of the audience, and divide them into:
  - Planned activities.
  - Procedures for covering possible crises – industrial accidents or product contaminations – as well as contingency plans for changes of government and takeover bids.

- Develop activities based on an agreed set of themes for the year. These might be supplier partnerships, quality improvements or safe working.

- Include clear guidelines on how to handle the media, and on how to support senior managers who may be called on as spokespeople; and formulate responses on public issues.

- Clarify the reporting mechanisms and put together an annual schedule of planning meetings and reviews, together with opportunities to feed creative ideas into the communication process.

- Measure performance against goals, and review the prominence of different areas.

- Refresh the quantitative research every so often with some qualitative research among key groups. This could include group discussions among employees or one-to-one interviews with customers, regulators, distributors, industry bodies and other opinion-formers. Whatever kind of research you do, it should be timed so that the results help formulate your communication objectives for the year ahead.

Summary – Refreshing the Planning Process

- The corporate communicator's prime role is to develop standards for communication.

- Effective standards depend on commonly accepted measurements, which can quantify progress made against set objectives.

- Research should feed the annual cycle for planning your communications, so that the needs of different audiences are understood and given the right priorities – and to make sure the agreed messages and themes are getting through.

19
Managing Reputation

A key theme of this book is that employees, customers and other external groups form their own judgement about an organization's reputation from a whole range of influences. These *orbits of experience* for employees include:

- Recruitment.

- Induction.

- Training and development.

- Their remuneration package.

- Values and behaviours experienced in different situations.

- Observations on the way other employees are treated.

- In-bred attitudes in the organization towards the groups it serves.

And for external groups these may include:

- The recommendation which brought them into contact.

- The experience of contacting the organization.

- Being sold to.

- Completing a transaction.

- Negotiating with the organization.

- Reading about it in the media.

- Complaining.

- Experiencing the organization's administration.

- Ending the relationship.

In the case of both employees and outside groups, reputations are formed in the eye of the beholders through a plethora of influences outside the control of any one person or department.

The human resource function does not exclusively control the perceptions of employees. Equally marketing or corporate communications do not control the perceptions of customers or other outsiders, like the media or community groups.

So it is clearly not possible to manage reputation by placing it solely in the hands of a particular specialism. Because reputation is the sum of experiences, it is the responsibility of everyone in the organization. It must be managed as a collective responsibility.

The reputation diagram reveals the links between the reputations that people perceive, as well as how the souls and strategies of organizations inter-relate with the experiences of employees and outsiders.

The role of professional communicators is to *facilitate* this realization and to create forums and processes that involve all employees in sharing responsibility for managing reputation.

This means that – as well as implementing communication programmes – the next generation of communicators must be chosen for their team working and managerial skills.

They will need to be able to design systems which engage colleagues in an annual communication planning process as well as day-by-day. The annual process is best illustrated by the communication planning cycle.

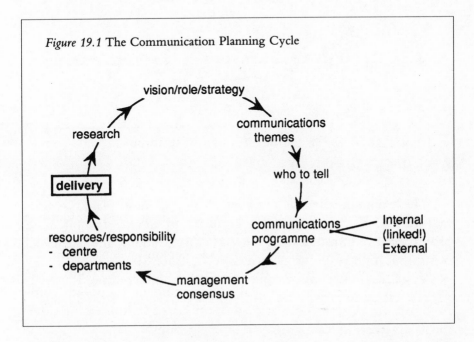

Figure 19.1 The Communication Planning Cycle

The circle diagram begins with research, to create a debate among managers, based on the organization's current reputation. At this debate, the big issues facing the organization should be identified and responses thrashed out which can be reflected in all the programmes proposed for the year.

Using the Communication Planning Calendar, professional communicators can ask colleagues to identify the big issues and activities which are likely to make news or provide an opportunity to communicate.

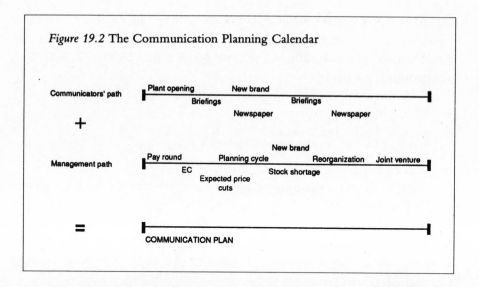

Figure 19.2 The Communication Planning Calendar

The planning calendar involves all managers in planning communication. To get colleagues involved in day-to-day planning, professional communicators should think about the issues-led communication planning described in Chapter Six.

Together these two simple concepts enable communicators to get reputation management firmly onto the management agenda.

SUMMARY – MANAGING REPUTATION

- Reputation is the sum of experiences of employees and external groups.

- Managing reputation means understanding the 'orbits' of experience of both employees and outsiders.

- It is not enough to manage image by itself. You must create a communication planning process which involves all managers and employees.

- Professional communicators must develop their skills as facilitators, and design annual and day-to-day processes involving other managers in managing the organization's reputation.

Index